TYGER

TYGER

A CELEBRATION

based on the life and work of
William Blake

ADRIAN MITCHELL

Music by
MIKE WESTBROOK

JONATHAN CAPE
THIRTY BEDFORD SQUARE LONDON

FIRST PUBLISHED 1971

© 1971 BY ADRIAN MITCHELL

JONATHAN CAPE LTD, 30 BEDFORD SQUARE, LONDON WCI

ISBN Paperback edition 0 224 00652 5
Hardback edition 0 224 00638 x

PRINTED AND BOUND IN GREAT BRITAIN
BY W & J MACKAY & CO LTD, CHATHAM

This play was first presented by the National Theatre at the New Theatre, London, on July 20th, 1971, under the direction of Michael Blakemore and John Dexter. The cast was as follows:

Isabelle	Isabelle Lucas
Klopstock	David Ryall
Sir Joshua Rat	John Moffatt
First Intellectual	David Kincaid
Second Intellectual	Tony Leary
Third Intellectual	James Hayes
Barmaid	Maggie Riley
William Blake	Gerald James
Scofield	Denis Quilley
Home Secretary	Anthony Nicholls
Civil Servant	Malcolm Reid
The Crab	Ian Burford
Kate Blake	Jane Wenham
The Revd Dr Trusler	Michael Turner
The Ghost of a Flea	Peter Smart
Postman	Anthony Barnett
First Randy Woman	Sarah Atkinson
Second Randy Woman	Maureen Lipman
Third Randy Woman	Louie Ramsay
Lord Nobodaddy	David Henry
Lady Twat	Hazel Hughes
Evelyn Graze	Malcolm Reid
Robert Southey	James Hayes
Mechanical Creature	Peter Duncan
Captain Stedman	Denis Lill
Henry Fuseli	Ray Callaghan

Samuel Palmer	John Gulliver
Geoffrey Chaucer	David Henry
William Shakespeare	Michael Turner
John Milton	David Ryall
William Wordsworth	Alan Jackson
Percy Bysshe Shelley	Dave Wintour
Samuel Coleridge	Riggs O'Hara
John Keats	Peter Duncan
Lord Byron	Norman Beaton
Alfred Lord Tennyson	Denis Lill
Robert Browning	David Kincaid
Walt Whitman	Bernard Gallagher
Edward Lear	James Hayes
Rudyard Kipling	Tony Leary
Allen Ginsberg	Ian Burford
Judge	Lewis Jones
Lawyer	Kenneth Mackintosh
King George	Bill Fraser
Working Man	Bernard Gallagher
Working Man's Wife	Mary Griffiths
Working Man's Family	Jean Boht
	Anthony Barnett
	Peter Duncan

CHARACTERS

ISABELLE, *a singer*
CHORUS OF MEN AND WOMEN
KLOPSTOCK, *a cultural middleman*
SIR JOSHUA RAT, *a portraitist*
BARMAID
THREE INTELLECTUALS
WILLIAM BLAKE
SCOFIELD, *a soldier*
HOME SECRETARY
CIVIL SERVANT
THE CRAB, *an informer*
KATE BLAKE, *wife of William*
THE REVD DR TRUSLER, *a patron*
THE GHOST OF A FLEA
TWO MEN IN WHITE COATS
POSTMAN
THREE RANDY WOMEN
LORD NOBODADDY, *Chairman, British Cultural Committee*
LADY TWAT
EVELYN GRAZE, *editor of literary magazine*
ROBERT SOUTHEY, *an ex-Communist*
MECHANICAL CREATURE
TWO PRISON WARDERS
CAPTAIN STEDMAN, *a decent English mercenary*
HENRY FUSELI
SAMUEL PALMER
GEOFFREY CHAUCER
WILLIAM SHAKESPEARE
JOHN MILTON

THE ROMANTIC REVIVAL:
  SAMUEL COLERIDGE
  WILLIAM WORDSWORTH
  JOHN KEATS
  PERCY BYSSHE SHELLEY
  LORD BYRON
RUDYARD KIPLING
ALFRED LORD TENNYSON
ROBERT BROWNING
WALT WHITMAN
EDWARD LEAR
ALLEN GINSBERG
CHORUS OF CRITICS
JUDGE
LAWYER
KING GEORGE
WORKING MAN *and his* WIFE *and* CHILDREN
CHORUS OF THE PEOPLE OF BRITAIN
SOLDIERS
A CHILD

SONGS

ACT ONE

ISABELLE *comes on alone.*
Music.

ISABELLE (*sings*).
　　I wander thro' each charter'd street,
　　Near where the charter'd Thames does flow,
　　And mark in every face I meet
　　Marks of weakness, marks of woe.

　　In every cry of every Man,
　　In every infant's cry of fear,
　　In every voice, in every ban,
　　The mind-forg'd manacles I hear.

　　How the Chimney-sweeper's cry
　　Every black'ning Church appalls;
　　And the hapless Soldier's sigh
　　Runs in blood down Palace walls.

　　But most thro' midnight streets I hear
　　How the youthful Harlot's curse
　　Blasts the new born Infant's tear,
　　And blights with plagues the Marriage hearse.
　　(CHORUS *enter set of* SIR JOSHUA RAT's *studio, strolling*
　　about the stage gloomily.)
CITIZEN ONE. Look!
CITIZEN TWO. Goodness gracious, isn't that Mr Klopstock
　　from the British Cultural Committee?
CITIZEN THREE. It certainly is. I've seen him on BBC-2 more
　　often than I've had hot dinners.
CHORUS. Hooray for Mr Klopstock.

(KLOPSTOCK, *a cultural middleman, youngish, in a superb suit, tap-dances to the centre of the stage.*)

CHORUS. Hooray! Hooray! Hooray!

KLOPSTOCK (*singing and tap-dancing*).

I've come from the British Cultural Committee.
Something must be done to electrify this city.
Of course we're all embarrassed by anything arty
But I'm sure you'll join in when I call for three hearty
Cheers for our host, who's going to give a chat –
The Henry Ford of portraiture – Sir Joshua Rat!
(SIR JOSHUA RAT, *in a small chariot whose panels are painted with allegories of a prim nature, is drawn around the stage by* CHORUS. SIR JOSHUA *wears modern morning-dress but a late-eighteenth-century wig. Wild enthusiasm. There is an easel with several canvases mounted in the chariot, and* SIR JOSHUA *wields a palette and brushes.*)

CHORUS (*sing*).

Three bloody cheers for Sir Joshua Rat
He could paint the portrait of a five pound note.
Always lays a bullet-proof undercoat
Before he does a picture of an aristocrat.

KLOPSTOCK. Ladies and gentlemen, Sir Joshua Rat has agreed to explain to us how he raised the status of the artist and his own standard of living in a series of fell swoops!

SIR JOSHUA (*sings*).

I was born on the healthier side of the tracks,
My father was a clergyman with skin like soap.
As a child I shook hands with Alexander Pope,
And I never never never looked back.

KLOPSTOCK (*sings*).

He's the friend of Lord Beaumont, Lord Bruce and Lord Downe,

CHORUS (*sing*).

He lives in St Martins Lane.

12

KLOPSTOCK (*sings*).
>He's painted all the statesmen, the literary gentry,

CHORUS (*sing*).
>And all the wealthy actresses in the town.

KLOPSTOCK (*shouts*). Tell the people how many pictures you've
done, Josh!

SIR JOSHUA (*sings*).
>One hundred and fifty portraits
>In Seventeen-Fifty-Eight alone;
>More than three thousand oils completed
>In thirty-six years of wearing my brush to the bone.

CHORUS (*sing*).
>Must be a record, yes, we'll drink to that.
>Must be a record for Sir Joshua Rat.

SIR JOSHUA (*sings*).
>The Duke of Devon, the Duke of Grafton,
>I painted in a simplified but dignified fashion.
>Sir James and Lady Colebrook, Lord Godolphin,
>And Diana personified by Lady Anna Dawson.
>(CHORUS *pose as the subjects of the portraits while* SIR
>JOSHUA *kisses their hands, sketches them, is given money, etc.*)

KLOPSTOCK (*sings*).
>Lord Stormont and Lord Huntingdon
>On the same canvas.
>The former Home Secretary –
>Lord Holderness.
>A full-length job
>On the Duchess of Hamilton.
>The Circumnavigator,
>Brave Lord Anson.
>General Guise,
>And pretty Miss Wynward –

SIR JOSHUA (*sings*).
>My old friends

Mr and Mrs Bastard.
Lord Bath, Lord Monford,
And Lady Kildare.
Sir William Lowther
The young millionaire.
David Garrick
In a Gielgud pose.
Horace Walpole
Nearly picking his nose.

CHORUS (*sing*).

The Duke of Ancaster
And Lord North.
Captain Orme
Upon a dubious horse.
The Prince of Wales
And the Duke of Sutherland.
The Hero of Culloden –
The Duke of Cumberland.
The Princess Augusta
And Lady May Coke.
Lady Sarah Bunbury
Enjoying a joke.

KLOPSTOCK (*sings*).

But what can we do with all these paintings to spare?

SIR JOSHUA (*sings*).

Why not found a Royal Academy and stick them in there?

CHORUS (*sing*).

Hooray! A Royal Academy!

SIR JOSHUA (*sings*).

But who'd be in charge of a palace like that?

KLOPSTOCK (*sings*).

Well, my vote goes to Sir Joshua Rat!

(CHORUS, *with an outbreak of 'Hoorays', chair* SIR JOSHUA
who is decorated with an impressive cloak by two girls from the

CHORUS *and a President-of-the-R.A.'s hat by* KLOP-
STOCK.)

SIR JOSHUA (*sings*).

Master Crew as a King, Master Herbert as Bacchus and
Master Cox as Hannibal,

Lord Sidney with a bow and arrow, Lord Althorpe sup-
ported by a pedestal,

Miss Jessie Cholomondley carrying a puppy across a
stretch of water.

The Duchess of Devonshire just about to clobber her
youngest daughter.

Lady Catherine Pelham-Clinton, Prince William of
Gloucester.

Lord Heathfield doing something with the key to
Gibraltar.

The Grand Old Duke of York and the Provost of Eton

And Colonel Tarlstone with his foot on a cannon.

(*Dances.*)

CHORUS (*sing*).

Three bloody cheers for Sir Joshua Rat,

Colour Photographer to the Great.

When you're dead you'll lie in state

In your President's robes and your President's hat.

(*A portable pulpit is pushed on. At the top is a frame like the one
round a TV screen.* SIR JOSHUA *mounts pulpit and mouths
silently from the screen. A bar comes on from the other side,
pushed by a* BARMAID, *also an open fireplace, over which
hangs a brass bed-warmer. Some of* CHORUS *take drinks and
become people in pub, with* THREE INTELLECTUALS *to the
fore.*)

FIRST INTELLECTUAL (*to* SECOND *and* THIRD INTELLEC-
TUALS). They say he was bent, but I don't believe it.

SECOND INTELLECTUAL. Are you telling me that Kit Marlowe was M.I.5?

15

THIRD INTELLECTUAL (*drunkenly*). Kit Marlowe and Rupert Brooke was like that. (*Tries to indicate this relationship with his fingers, doesn't believe himself.*)

FIRST INTELLECTUAL. Mind if I turn up the sound on the box, Gladys?

SECOND INTELLECTUAL. Yeah, it's Sir Joshua Rat giving the 27th of one hundred and forty four discourses on Western Cutlery.

> (FIRST INTELLECTUAL *turns up the sound. The* THREE INTELLECTUALS *gather round reverently.*)

SIR JOSHUA. Compared with the true splendour of Nature, the best coloured pictures are but faint and feeble.

BLAKE (*emerging from audience*). Nonsense! Every eye sees differently.

BARMAID. Evening, Mr Blake. The usual, is it?

> (BLAKE *nods as he walks to the bar.* BARMAID *pulls him a two pint transparent tankard of golden liquid illuminated from within.*)

BLAKE. Cheers.

SIR JOSHUA. A student examines his own mind and perceives there nothing of that divine inspiration with which, he is told, so many others have been favoured.

BLAKE. The man who on examining his own mind finds nothing of inspiration ought not to dare to be an artist.

SIR JOSHUA. Most people err, not so much from want of capacity to find their object, as from not knowing what object to pursue.

BLAKE. The man who does not know what object to pursue is an idiot.

SECOND INTELLECTUAL. Fair play. He's not in a position to answer back.

SIR JOSHUA. As I have formerly observed, enthusiastic admiration seldom promotes knowledge.

BLAKE (*noisily*). Enthusiastic admiration is the first principle of knowledge and it's last. Now he begins to degrade, to deny and to mock.

SIR JOSHUA. If you mean to preserve the most perfect beauty in its most perfect state, you cannot express the passions.

BLAKE (*approaching the set, tankard in hand*). Passion and expression is beauty itself. The face that is incapable of passion and expression is deformity itself. Let it be painted and patched and praised and advertised for ever, it will only be admired by fools.

FIRST INTELLECTUAL. He's not the President of the Royal Academy for nothing, mind.

BLAKE (*turning on him*). I have spent the vigour of my youth and genius under the oppression of Sir Joshua and his gang of cunning hired knaves.

FIRST INTELLECTUAL. He knows what he's on about.

BLAKE. The mischief is just the same whether a man does it ignorantly or knowingly. Such artists as the Rat are at all times hired for the depression of art – a pretence of art to destroy art.

FIRST INTELLECTUAL. If you know so much, why aren't you on the telly?

SECOND INTELLECTUAL. If you're so honest, why aren't you in jail?

THIRD INTELLECTUAL. If you're so revolutionary, why aren't you dead?

BLAKE. The inquiry in England is not whether a man has talents and genius, but whether he is passive and polite and a virtuous ass and obedient to noblemen's opinions in art and science. If he is, he is a good man. If not, he must be starved.

SIR JOSHUA (*expostulating*). After so much has been done for artists by the British Cultural Committee –

BLAKE. Three farthings! This man was hired to depress art.

 (BLAKE *hurls the remains of his drink in* SIR JOSHUA'*s face.*

SIR JOSHUA *stays in the screen, dripping.*)
BARMAID. Billy Blake, you've gone too far again.
FIRST INTELLECTUAL. We're going to give you a little discourse with our boots.
SECOND INTELLECTUAL. We're going to waltz you twice round the car park.
THIRD INTELLECTUAL. We're going to culture you into the tarmac.

(*The* THREE INTELLECTUALS *advance on* BLAKE, *beginning to take off their jackets. Before their jackets are off,* BLAKE *charges, head down, and butts* FIRST INTELLECTUAL *into* SECOND INTELLECTUAL. THIRD INTELLECTUAL *avoids falling as they go down, and* BLAKE *stands over them.* THIRD INTELLECTUAL *sidles over to* BARMAID, *who hands him a bottle. He tries to creep up behind* BLAKE *to smash his head, but* BLAKE, *without turning round, kicks back a barstool which trips* THIRD INTELLECTUAL. BLAKE *picks from the wall the bed-warmer, which has a long handle. On the handle is a lever which opens and shuts the mouth of the bed-warmer.* BLAKE *stands with his back to the fire, threatening with the bed-warmer any of his opponents who attempt to get up.*
BARMAID (*calling upstairs*). Hey, Scofey! Down here a minute.
SCOFIELD (*sleepily off*). Wharramarrer?
BARMAID. Artistic controversy.
SCOFIELD (*off*). Awright. Jesus Iscariot!

(SCOFIELD, *a very large Army private, paratrooper, comes in blearily, webbing belt in his hand.* BARMAID *motions to* BLAKE *with her head.* SCOFIELD *and* BLAKE *sum each other up,* SCOFIELD *grinning slowly.*)
Right, squire, I think it's time you crawled back to your cave.
BLAKE. You a soldier?
SCOFIELD. Oh, you don't even know a British soldier when you see one, eh?
BLAKE. I know the difference between a maker and a murderer.

SCOFIELD. Well, that's a start, isn't it, but where's it going to finish?

FIRST INTELLECTUAL. Want to watch him. He's harder than he looks. Does a sort of Zen karate.

SECOND INTELLECTUAL. He'll have a go at anyone. Remember the time he done up Rubens?

SCOFIELD. I'm a soldier. What the raving hell are you?

BLAKE. I'm William Blake. I paint and I write poems.

SCOFIELD. Well, my name's 6483329 Scofield, and if it wasn't for buggers like me, buggers like you wouldn't be able to talk to buggers like me. We've been bleeding to death in every bleeding country in the world for your free bleeding speech so shut your bleeding trap when you talk to me. But you don't give a buttered turd for blokes like me, do you? You don't give a throbbin' thank you for all the protection you get from us soldier boys, do you?

BLAKE. Look, I'm against all kinds of slavery. But if a man chooses to be a slave – good luck to him. And don't tell me about protection. I've lived most of my life in Soho.

SCOFIELD. Right. That's it, then. Gladys. Pass me Montgomery, if you'd be so kind.

(BARMAID *climbs on a stool and fetches down a shotgun, passes it down to* SCOFIELD, *who makes sure it's loaded and advances, aiming it at* BLAKE. *But during this business,* BLAKE *has levered open his warming-pan, pushed it into the fire so that it is full of hot coals, levered it closed again, and hoisted it into the air. So when the two men confront each other, the warming-pan full of hot coals is directly over* SCOFIELD'*s head, and* BLAKE *has it half open, so that at any point he could drop the coals. Stalemate, in fact.* BLAKE *then manoeuvres round and backs towards the door.*)

BLAKE. Drop that gun, or I'll roast you.

SCOFIELD (*lowering the gun*). Bloody aerial warfare, that's what it is. Right. But one fine night I'll get you up an alley and

then we'll play school. And I'll be the bleeding teacher –
(BLAKE *begins to exit through orchestra.*)

SCOFIELD (*to* BARMAID). Full retreat, eh? Retired in disorder?

BARMAID. I'd have bashed him, personally.

SCOFIELD. Gladys, get me the Home Office on the buzzer. There's more ways than one of tearing the skin off a man's back. Don't you fret, Glad, one of these mornings he'll find himself upside down on the municipal dump with his engine took out. But first we might try a little discreet lynching.

BLAKE (*sings from orchestra pit*).
When Sir Joshua Reynolds died
All Nature was degraded;
The King drop'd a tear in the Queen's Ear,
And all his Pictures Faded.
(*Exit* BLAKE. *Scene changes to the Home Office. The* HOME SECRETARY *sits at his desk, telephone to his ear. There is a large metal filing cabinet beside him.*)

HOME SECRETARY. Thanks, Private Scofield. We've heard rumours about this Blake, but we thought he'd been ignored to death some time ago. Keep up the good work.
(HOME SECRETARY *puts down phone, pulls out top drawer of filing cabinet. The head of a* CIVIL SERVANT *emerges from the drawer.*)
What've we got on William Blake?

CIVIL SERVANT. Ba, bb, bc, be, bf, bg, bh, bi, bj, bk, bl, bla, bla, bla, Blake. Blake, William. Engraver. Married, no children, lives London, writes rigmarole about French and American revolutions. Maybe subversive rigmarole. Under loose watch by the Media Police.

HOME SECRETARY. Better investigate him. Who's the sneakiest spy on standby tonight?

CIVIL SERVANT. James Bond's defected to South Africa. And Batman's campaigning for Ronald Reagan.

HOME SECRETARY. Hm. That only leaves –

CIVIL SERVANT. – the Crab.

> (*The* CRAB, *who has been lurking under the desk, emerges.*
> *He wears green tweeds and a green tweed hat, is very shifty*
> *and usually moves sideways.*)

HOME SECRETARY. Ah, there you are, Crab, disgusting as
ever. I'd like you to sidle down to Soho and suss out a hack
called Blake. Just a casual examination, you understand, to
ascertain whether the balance of his mind is such as to
endanger the public peace of mind, cause an obstruction or
lead to a breach of the war.

CRAB. But Home Secretary, sir, can't you give me a clean little
job for a change? All these slimy assignments, they're
affecting my metabolism. There's a permanent waterfall of
cold sweat down my backbone, sir.

HOME SECRETARY. I know, it's an old story, Crab. But what
do you expect to earn by working for the Home Office? A
nickel halo?

CRAB. No, sir, it's not that I'm going human or anything. Just –
you always put me on the small fry – artists, writers, newspaper vendors. If only you'd send me after someone really
dangerous, like Bernadette Devlin –

HOME SECRETARY. Don't underestimate culture, Crab.
Empire against art, remember?

CRAB. But I even like some of them, sir, I even like some of their
work.

HOME SECRETARY. You have qualms? Is this the same Crab
who put the bite on W. H. Auden until he turned religious?
The Crab who bought a 51 per cent controlling interest in
Alfred Lord Tennyson and punctured Shelley's water-
wings? Here, take a hundred oncers. (*Gives* CRAB *a bundle*
of notes.) Get after Blake. Remember, we want him certified,
straitjacketed, signed, sealed and delivered in a plain black
van by the first Good Friday on your right.

CRAB. Yours obediently, the Crab.

> (*Scene changes to* BLAKE's *workroom.* BLAKE *is at work, sketching.* KATE BLAKE, *his wife, comes down the stairs. She is gentle and practical.* BLAKE *works on, then stops and, still looking at his sketch, takes her hand and draws her to his side. They both look at the sketch.*)

BLAKE. I saw Robert.

KATE. Robert who?

BLAKE. Robert, my brother.

KATE. William!

BLAKE. Yes, I know he's dead but he came in our bedroom in the middle of the night and he showed me how I can print all those poems properly, with leaves entwined between the lines and flying figures swooping among the stanzas and great rocks in the corners – every poem a painting and every painting a stained-glass window made of paper. Look, first I write out the verse and the designs and the bits in the margin – I outline them on copper with some impervious liquid, ordinary stopping-out varnish should do. Then all the white parts of the plate will be eaten away with aqua fortis or some other acid. So all that's left is the outline of the design. We can take these plates and print them off in any colour we want. That's the outline, that's what matters. Then we colour up the pages by hand.

KATE. We've got some old copper plates, but –

BLAKE. We've got a half-crown too. Nip out and get the varnish and the acid.

KATE. But it's all the money we've got.

BLAKE. Oh, damn the money, it's always the money.

KATE (*grins*). I'm off.

> (KATE *goes, taking half-crown.* BLAKE *settles down to sketch. An empty chair is in front of him. Knock at the door.*)

BLAKE. Come in if you must.

> (*Enter* DR TRUSLER, *an elderly clergyman. Forbidding*

aspect, dark and tall, holding at arm's length a Blake design.)
Good morning.

TRUSLER. Sir, here is the illustration I commissioned from you.
And yet, sir, this is not the illustration I commissioned from
you.

BLAKE. Must've been using my imagination again.

TRUSLER. Sir, it appears to me that you cannot draw people.

BLAKE. I can draw *my* people.

TRUSLER. But men don't have straining muscles all over their
backs and thighs. And women don't have golden ligaments
and golden breasts. There aren't any people like that.

BLAKE. There are now.

TRUSLER. And even if there were, you couldn't see all those
lines through people's clothes.

BLAKE. Just look through the clothes. And then look through
the skin. And there are the lines.

TRUSLER. This is fantasy. I am not a man for fantasy. I shall
withhold my fee.

(BLAKE *strides forward and pushes him into a chair.*)

BLAKE. But you ought to know that what is grand is necessarily
obscure to weak men. That which can be made explicit to
the idiot is not worth my care.

TRUSLER (*attempting to rise*). But your anatomy's thoroughly
distorted, sir.

BLAKE (*sings*).

I feel that a man may be happy in This World.
And I know that This World
Is a World of imagination & Vision.
I see All I Paint In This World,
But Every body does not see alike.
To the Eyes of a Miser a Guinea
Is more beautiful than the Sun,
& a bag worn with the use of Money
Has more beautiful proportions

Than a Vine filled with Grapes.
The tree which moves some to tears of joy
Is in the Eyes of others
Only a Green thing that stands in the way.

TRUSLER. But I'm most unhappy to find –

BLAKE. But I am happy to find a great majority of fellow mortals who can elucidate my visions, and particularly they have been elucidated by children, who have taken a greater delight in contemplating my pictures than I ever hoped. Neither youth nor childhood is folly or incapacity. Some children are fools, and so are some old men. But there is a vast majority on the side of imagination or spiritual sensation.

(KATE *re-enters, during this, with a bottle of acid and another of varnish.*)

KATE. Eightpence change, William, and that's our life savings. Lovely morning, isn't it, Mr Trusler?

TRUSLER (*rising, as* BLAKE *turns to take the bottles*). What public reputation you have, the reputation of eccentricity excepted, I have acquired for you. But the public is willing to give you credit for what real talent is to be found in your productions, and for no more. I was determined to bring you food as well as reputation, though from your late conduct, I have reason to embrace the opinion that, to manage genius, and to cause it to produce good things, it is absolutely necessary to starve it. Indeed, your best work was produced when you and Mrs Blake were reduced so low as to be obliged to live on half a guinea a week!

BLAKE (*staring at him*). I wonder who made you?

(TRUSLER *begins to retreat under the evil eye.*)

I wonder who made you? I wonder who made you?

(*Exit* TRUSLER. BLAKE *stares after him.*)

KATE. Forget him, William, forget him quickly. No use brooding about *them*.

BLAKE. You're right. It's not useful.

KATE. Then stop it.

(BLAKE *draws the palm of his hand slowly, twice, across his forehead.*)

BLAKE. Yes. I'm trying. Wiping him out of my head. He's fading. He's fading. He's gone.

KATE. Sure?

(BLAKE *nods.*)

Then I'll make the lunch.

(KATE *exits.* BLAKE *returns to his sketching. A knock at the door.*)

BLAKE. Who's there?

CRAB (*outside*). An artistic connoisseur.

BLAKE. Why don't you go back where you came from?

CRAB (*through half-open door*). Allow me to wheedle you, Mr Blake. I'm an art-lover, an art-angel and an art-licker.

BLAKE. Give the password.

CRAB. Up the French Revolution.

BLAKE. That's a start.

CRAB. Long live the American Revolution.

BLAKE. Right so far. Carry on.

CRAB (*with a gulp*). Roll on the British Revolution.

BLAKE (*opening the door*). You'll do. Sit down, not in that chair. Sit down, shut up, I'm working.

CRAB. It must be wonderful to be –

BLAKE. Quiet, she's back again.

CRAB. Who? Where?

BLAKE (*pointing at empty chair*). Haven't you met Corinna? She won the gold medal for gold at the Olympics.

CRAB. Might I see some of your new work?

(BLAKE *looks at him, nods, goes over and switches on slide projector. Slide of the Builder of the Pyramids.*)

BLAKE. What d'you think that is?

CRAB (*looking at drawing*). He seems rather unpleasant.

BLAKE. He's a right bastard. He was foreman when they were building the pyramids. Came and sat for me last March. Who's this?

(*Slide of Satan.*)

CRAB. Some distinguished personage?

BLAKE. Satan. Not bad of him really. Cross between a supernatural Air Vice-Marshal and a police informer.

CRAB. Er, yes, very compelling. D'you mind if I ask you a few questions?

BLAKE (*standing up*). Ask away, you'll find I'm a pretty harmless nut.

CRAB. Not at all. What do you think of Socrates?

BLAKE. I was Socrates. A sort of brother. I must have talked with him. And Jesus too. I seem to remember being with both of them.

CRAB. Do you believe in the divinity of Jesus?

BLAKE. Jesus Christ is the only God.

(CRAB *grins and nods.*)

And so am I ... (*to audience*) And so are you. (*To* CRAB) And so are you.

(CRAB *paces round in a small circle, then looks at* BLAKE.)

CRAB. Where do you stand on education?

BLAKE. I stand on lack of education. Never had any. Couldn't use it. Education's wrong. It's the great sin. Look at Plato, all he knew about was the virtues and vices of good and evil. There's nothing in all that. Everything's good in God's eyes.

CRAB. But I thought you said I was God.

BLAKE. You are, but your eyes are half shut and gummed up.

CRAB. How wonderful it must be to see visions.

BLAKE. Everyone has the power to see visions. But they lose it because they don't work on it. Now I'll show you one last portrait.

(*Slide of 'The Ghost of a Flea'.*)

What do you think of it?

CRAB. I see a naked figure with a strong body and a short neck –
with burning eyes which long for moisture, and a face
worthy of a murderer, holding a cup of blood in its clawed
hands, out of which it seems eager to drink.

BLAKE. God Save the King.

CRAB. But what in the world is it?

BLAKE. It's a ghost. The ghost of a flea. I wish I'd been able to
draw his mouth properly. Ah, here he comes again. Quick,
pass my pencil, I'll get that mouth now.

(CRAB *passes a pencil and watches* BLAKE's *paper as he
begins to draw. But* BLAKE *stares up, smiling slightly, at the
figure of the* GHOST OF A FLEA, *based on* BLAKE's *detailed
portrait, as it stalks into the room.*)

Here he comes. Look at his tongue whisking out of his
mouth. There's the cup in his hand, ready to hold the blood.
Must get this down.

CRAB. What a picturesque fancy! Why I could –

(*As* BLAKE *draws, the* GHOST OF A FLEA *menaces* CRAB,
*who sees it, looks back to the drawing to check its likeness, is
impressed, then double-takes, leaps in the air and is chased by
the* GHOST OF A FLEA *out of the workroom.*

KATE BLAKE *comes in with a mug and a bottle of wine and
puts it on the table by* BLAKE. BLAKE *puts one arm round her
waist as he finishes his drawing.*)

KATE (*looking at drawing*). Doodling again.

BLAKE. Yes, but it's a good doodle, isn't it Kate? As doodles go.

KATE. Yes. Who were you talking to just now?

BLAKE. Bloody M.I.5 again.

KATE. How'd you get rid of him?

BLAKE. I set Freddy on to him.

(*Scene changes back to the Home Office.* HOME SECRETARY
at desk. CRAB *enters in a muck sweat.*)

HOME SECRETARY. What's the dirt on Blake?

CRAB. Well, it was a bad time to call because he had this Ancient

Roman whore who won the Olympics sitting for him, and he'd been having a quick word with Jesus, who is me as it turns out, but Socrates turned him on to hemlock and then he got a phone call from Voltaire only it was reverse charges from the grave and the real trouble with Blake is that one day he was sitting under an electric tree and Milton was perched on one of the branches, but then Milton got ripe and fell on Blake's head.

HOME SECRETARY. I see. So you made an excuse and left. (*Presses a desk buzzer.*)

CRAB. Not exactly. He said I was God, but he was God too. And you too, of course, Home Secretary.

HOME SECRETARY. How cosy. So you stayed.

CRAB. Well I would've stayed. Nobody ever called me God before. But then he brought in this great bulging monster.

HOME SECRETARY. Any specific design of monster?

CRAB. It was the Ghost of a Flea.

HOME SECRETARY. The Ghost of a Flea? Really, Crab, I am examining my wrists for goose pimples, yet I can find none.

(TWO MEN IN WHITE COATS *creep up behind* CRAB.)

CRAB. Yes, but it was a six-foot-something flea with a cup to catch the blood and –

(CRAB *is grabbed and lugged off by the* TWO MEN IN WHITE COATS. HOME SECRETARY *opens filing cabinet drawer.* CIVIL SERVANT *looks out.*)

HOME SECRETARY. Better try a slightly different tack on this Blake. We've ignored him for years and he just pushes on with his work. He's never had a review yet, let's try some constructive criticism on him.

CIVIL SERVANT. Crab, crap, crass, cretin, cri, cri, critic, criticism. Criticism of Blake Exhibition suitable to be published in *The Examiner* of 1809 –

HOME SECRETARY. That'll do nicely. How does it go?

CIVIL SERVANT (*rapidly*). When the ebullitions of a distem-

28

pered brain are mistaken for the sallies of genius, the malady has indeed attained a most pernicious height, and it becomes a duty to endeavour to arrest its progress. Such is the case with the productions and admirers of William Blake, an unfortunate lunatic whose personal inoffensiveness secures him from confinement.

HOME SECRETARY. I like it, I like it.

(*The* GHOST OF A FLEA *enters and creeps up behind* HOME SECRETARY.)

CIVIL SERVANT (*ecstatically*). Thus encouraged, the poor man fancies himself a great master, and has painted a few wretched pictures, some unintelligible allegory, others an attempt at character representation, and the whole, blotted and blurred and very badly drawn. These he calls an exhibition, of which he has published a catalogue, or rather a farrago of nonsense, unintelligibleness and egregious vanity, the wild effusions of a distempered brain –

HOME SECRETARY (*by this time highly delighted*). That's his first review and it'll be the last. I'll send a copy to the *Statesman*. (*Sees the* GHOST OF A FLEA.) I say, you're not from the *Sunday Express*, are you?

(*The* GHOST OF A FLEA *opens its spectacular mouth and roars*.)

GHOST. Aaragh!

(GHOST *forces* HOME SECRETARY *over desk and begins to drink his blood. Scene changes to the* BLAKE'S *bedroom, which is raised above stage and has steps leading down to workroom.* BLAKE *and* KATE *in bed.* BLAKE *expansive, relaxed.* KATE *huddled, like an embryo, her back to him.*)

BLAKE. The head, sublime. The heart, pathos. The genitals, beauty. The hands and feet, proportion. I'm out of prison and into the sun. Where are you, Kate?

KATE. Over here in the wet bit.

BLAKE. The pride of the peacock is the glory of God. The lust of the goat is the bounty of God. The wrath of the lion is the wisdom of God. The nakedness of woman is the work of God. You love me, Kate.

KATE. Of course I love you. As well as I can.

BLAKE. Free again! Melted again!

KATE. I'm glad.

BLAKE. What's the matter?

KATE. *You're* free again. Nothing's the matter.

BLAKE. It can't be right or you wouldn't use a word like 'nothing'. An empty word. Anyway it can't be right, or we'd do it more often.

KATE. Too often I'm too tired.

BLAKE. How can you be too tired?

KATE. It's different for me. It doesn't set me free.

(BLAKE *angrily hurls himself out of bed, stomps down the stairs and begins to type at his table.* KATE *sits up in bed with a newspaper in her hands. She reads from newspaper ads.*)

'Energy is eternal delight. Poet, printer and prophet would like to meet randy women. Object: the lineaments of gratified desire. Box 505.'

(A POSTMAN *wheels a big crate marked 'Box 505' to* BLAKE'*s desk.* BLAKE *tips him. Exit* POSTMAN. *Sides of box open to disclose* THREE RANDY WOMEN.)

FIRST RANDY WOMAN (*sings*).

Dear Box Five Hundred and Five
I've got so much to give
My friends and enemies agree
I'm oversensitive.
The touch of a shadow
Puts my body in a shudder.
I can read in the dark with my thumb.
I'm so sexually aware
That a leather armchair
Makes me come and come and come.

(SECOND RANDY WOMAN *advances in similar way*.)
SECOND RANDY WOMAN (*sings*).
    Box Five-O-Five, I'm a buxom widow.
    I sleep on sheepskin with my arse out the window.
    I need a bronco buster
    To get his foot in my stirrup
    'Cos I'm randy
    Like brandy
    And I flow like golden syrup.
    Come on, bronco buster,
    Get your foot in my stirrup.
    (THIRD RANDY WOMAN *advances*.)
THIRD RANDY WOMAN (*sings*).
    Five-O-Five, I'm a sockaway rockaway wench.
    I can make it on a tightrope or a corporation bench.
    I'm not just one of your sexual freaks
    But I've won prizes for the following techniques –
    The Footsole Throbaway,
    The Rockinghorse Humjob,
    The Olive Oil Helter-Skelter,
    The Silverside Jump,
    The Warm Swarm,
    The Summertime Stoop
    And the Velvet-lined Deep Shelter.
    I can take out your appendix without an incision.
    I can make a half-arsed Andy Pandy come on like a
        Panzer Division.
    If you can pass all these and a few other simple tests
    I'll lullaby you by playing the Bells of St Mary's
    With my breasts.
THREE RANDY WOMEN (*sing*).
    Box Five Hundred and Five
    We know
    You feel like a wooden cube

Box Five Hundred and Five
We could turn you
Into a golden globe
So you can roll
Let your soul roll
Let your soul roll
Roll away.

BLAKE. As judge and jury of this sensational contest to choose
Miss Albion, I confess I'm as baffled as a zebra in St Paul's
Cathedral. You're all hired.

(THREE RANDY WOMEN *utter squeals of delight.*)

But before we work out a rota, I'd like you to meet my
open-minded wife.

(KATE *enters, a large frying pan behind her back.*)

Kate, I've got a little surprise for you. I'd like you to meet
these three randy women. They're going to lend a hand
and so on with our sex life.

KATE. Delighted, I'm sure.

(KATE *belabours the* THREE RANDY WOMEN *with her
frying-pan. They flee with outraged cries.*)

Delighted, I'm sure! Delighted, I'm sure! Delighted, I'm
sure!

BLAKE. Kate! You didn't need to smite them hip and thigh. I
started it all.

KATE. Instead of calling in that tatterdemalion, furlined Fire
Brigade, why didn't you learn how to turn *me* on?

BLAKE. Didn't know how to. Didn't know it could be done.

KATE. I'm not the Mona bloody Lisa.

BLAKE. I'll try. But you'll have to tell me how to get you going.

KATE. It's to do with tickling, really.

(BLAKE *tries tickling her ribs. She pulls away.*)

Not my ribs, you visionary buffoon.

BLAKE. What am I supposed to tickle, then?

KATE. That's the trouble. I don't know what it's called.

BLAKE. What what's called?

KATE. The starter button. I don't know what the damn thing's called.

(BLAKE *rushes to the side of the stage, returns with a bulky volume.*)

BLAKE. There you are. Gray's *Anatomy*. You could look it up. Should be on page 354. (*He flips through book, finds page and shows it to her.*)

KATE. Let's see. No, that's upside down. There. That's it. That's where my nerve-ends have their Clapham Junction.

BLAKE. Let's see. What, that little bud thing?

KATE. That's it. What does Gray call it?

BLAKE. It doesn't look much like yours. It doesn't look like much at all. It says it's called a clitoris.

KATE. That'll be it. Clitoris! That's the flower to go for!

BLAKE. I don't mind having a look for it, anyway.

KATE (*leading him upstairs*). Oh, I know where it is. I just didn't know its name.

(BLAKE *follows her up the stairs, consulting the book as he does so, puzzled, but willing to oblige.* CHORUS OF MEN *advance from one side of the stage.* CHORUS OF WOMEN *advance from the other side. They sing, not solemnly but cheerfully, not formally, more like high-spirited gospel singers.*)

WOMEN (*sing*).

What is it men in women do require?

MEN (*sing*).

The lineaments of gratified desire.

What is it women do in men require?

WOMEN (*sing*).

The lineaments of gratified desire.

What is it men in women do require?

MEN (*sing*).

The lineaments of gratified desire.

What is it women do in men require?

WOMEN (*sing*).

The lineaments of gratified desire.

(*This can be repeated, increasing in volume and richness until it's an explosion of sound. When it ends, CHORUS leave and KATE and BLAKE come down the stairs. Both of them look peaceful. KATE holds a baby in her arms. KATE sits. BLAKE smiles.*)

KATE. You can burp him now.

(*BLAKE nods, takes the baby, supporting its head carefully. He places the baby so that its belly is pressed against his shoulder. He rubs its back, then he smiles at KATE and nods to indicate that the baby has burped. Then he cradles the baby in his arms and looks at it. He hums to it. SIR JOSHUA comes on, in something of a rage, and appeals to the audience.*)

SIR JOSHUA. This is outrageous. Beyond everything.

Everyone knows Blake had no offspring.

This is no mere anachronism.

But a spanner in the computer of scholasticism.

No children were born to William Blake –

KATE. It takes a fake to spot a fake.

But you're wrong, Sir Joshua –

SIR JOSHUA. – and history's wrong?

KATE. Yes, history is very wrong.

Ask all the murdered people and see what
answer you get.

But history hasn't finished yet.

You can't understand our future or our past.

This is not our first child, nor our last.

SIR JOSHUA. Somerset House says that no births occurred.

KATE. You think we'd have our children registered?

(*SIR JOSHUA stamps off in fury.*)

(*sings, while BLAKE dances gently with the baby.*)

The children of Blake dance in their thousands

Over nursery meadows and through the sinister forests,

34

Beyond the spikes of cities, over the breasts of mountains,
The children of Blake dance in their thousands.
They dance beyond logic, they dance beyond science,
They are dancers, they are only dancers,
And every atom of their minds and hearts and their deep
skins
And every atom of their bowels and genitals and
imaginations
Dances to the music of William Blake.

(KATE *sits at the table, and begins to paint delicately in a small illuminated book.* BLAKE, *still holding the baby, looks over her shoulder.*)

KATE. I like him.

BLAKE. He's just a baby.

KATE (*pointing to book*). No, this tiger you engraved. But he looks worried.

BLAKE. Course he does. You're not copying the colours properly. Look, the shadow on this tree should be a happier kind of blue, look, it ought to reflect the blue in the top left-hand corner. All right?

KATE. All right.

BLAKE. Oh Kate, could you go out again and get me some paints? I need some indigo, cobalt, gamboge, vermilion, Frankfort black and ultramarine.

KATE. We've only got eightpence, remember?

BLAKE (*tense and angry*). All I want to do is work.

KATE. Why don't you apply for a grant to the British Cultural Committee? They're meant to help artists.

BLAKE. Like landlords help tenants.

KATE. You could try.

(BLAKE *kisses her, gives her the baby.*)

BLAKE. Work on that shadow, love. I'll go and try for a grant.

(*Exit* BLAKE. KATE, *with baby, goes to the workbench, looks at book, looks at baby, and sings* 'The Children of Blake' *as workroom is taken out. Scene changes to the boardroom of the British Cultural Committee. Banner descends, an elaborate one with 'British Cultural Committee' embroidered on it. A long table. At one end of it, a large In Tray, an Out Tray at the other end.* LORD NOBODADDY, *a grey-haired man in a grey suit, sits in a dark chairman's chair at the centre of the table. On his right sits* SIR JOSHUA RAT. *On his left,* KLOPSTOCK. *Beside the In Tray,* LADY TWAT, *an amateur author and censor.*)

NOBODADDY. Right, are we all here? Klopstock?

KLOPSTOCK. Sir.

NOBODADDY. Sir Joshua Rat?

SIR JOSHUA. Present and correct.

NOBODADDY. Lady Twat?

LADY TWAT. You *know* I'm here.

NOBODADDY. Lord Nobodaddy? Yes, I'm here. But I like the sound of me name. Right, we'd better mull over these munificent grants. Who's the first humble applicant? Ah, yes, Evelyn Graze.

(NOBODADDY *picks a letter from his papers.* EVELYN GRAZE *rises mysteriously from the In Tray. She is glamorous and intellectual and dresses to suit the part, but has an odd touch of the female impersonator.*)

EVELYN GRAZE (*sings*).

For the past two years
My friends and I have been
Editing a literary
Magazine.

Our list of contents
Should convince you that
We're always reliable
But never old hat:–

A fine novella
On the search
For identity
Translated
Into Ancient Norse
By a Downing Fellow
In the Church
Who was sent to me
Following my last divorce.

A sonnet on the lobster,
A photo of Pope Joan,
A survey on the mobster
From Creon to Capone.

But despite the generosity
Of the sugar industry
In taking advertising space,
I find it hard financially
To meet my sister's salary
And the rent and rates in St James's Place.

Now I know that belles lettres mean a great deal to you,
And seven thousand every year would see me through.
So do it for culture,
Do it for literature,
Do it for – Mummy!
Yours most sincerely, Evelyn Graze.
(*Poses enticingly and awaits the verdict.*)
NOBODADDY. I should say this looks like a clean-cut, clear-cut,
open and shut, black-and-white case.
SIR JOSHUA. Responsible, responsible.
KLOPSTOCK. Know where you are with a person like that.
SIR JOSHUA. That's right, Klopstock, responsible, responsible.
LADY TWAT. I was rather worried by the January issue. Did

you see the vignette in the January issue?

SIR JOSHUA. Responsible, yes. Responsible, yes.

NOBODADDY. What about the vignette in the January issue?

LADY TWAT. It used that word.

NOBODADDY. What word?

LADY TWAT. It used that word – cock.

NOBODADDY. What, Lady Twat?

LADY TWAT. Cock.

NOBODADDY. Cock, Lady Twat?

LADY TWAT. Cock cock cock cock. It used the word cock.

NOBODADDY. In the vignette?

LADY TWAT. In the January issue.

KLOPSTOCK (*producing magazine*). But that was in a vignette
called (*sonorously*) 'Les Amis Plumés d'une Ferme du Moyen
Age'. (*Translating for the benefit of B.C.C. – flatly.*) Feathered
friends on an old farm.

　　(*Members of B.C.C. laugh.*)

LADY TWAT. Well, that's quite different, quite quite different.

KLOPSTOCK. Know where you are with a vignette like that.

LADY TWAT. I didn't read the title. Didn't read the vignette.
But the word just jumped off the page and hit me. Cock!
Just like that.

SIR JOSHUA (*jocular*). Cock-a-doodle-doo!

KLOPSTOCK. Know where you are with a creature like that.

NOBODADDY. Still, it does rather jump off the page and hit
one. Just a bit careless of Evelyn, just a bit thoughtless.
Ought to have thought about people not reading through
the whole vignette.

KLOPSTOCK. Don't know where you are with a word like that.

SIR JOSHUA. Irresponsible? Irresponsible?

NOBODADDY. We could send a memo.

SIR JOSHUA. Yes, let's send a memo. Attach it to the cheque.

KLOPSTOCK. They'll know where they stand with a memo like
that.

38

NOBODADDY (*producing cheque book*). I suggest, and it's only a suggestion, mind, a mild memo paperclipped to a banker's order for ten thousand pounds per annum domino.

LADY TWAT. Excellent thinking.

SIR JOSHUA. Responsible thinking.

KLOPSTOCK. Know where you are with money like that.

NOBODADDY. All in favour, signify in the usual way.

(SIR JOSHUA, KLOPSTOCK, NOBODADDY *and* LADY TWAT *hurl themselves into a rapid-fire orgy of groping, thrusting, back-scratching, feeling and puffing. Scrum breaks up as suddenly as it began.*)

Unanimous again!

(NOBODADDY *writes out a cheque and hands it to* EVELYN GRAZE, *who unfreezes and begins to walk down the table shaking hands amorously with each Committee member in turn.*)

EVELYN GRAZE. Bless you! Bless you! You're all so gracious.

LADY TWAT. Cock indeed! Cock! I'm almost getting used to it.

SIR JOSHUA. Ambiguous, no. Ambiguous, yes.

KLOPSTOCK. Know where I stand with a chap like you.

NOBODADDY. I'll be round tonight for my Turtle Maryland.

EVELYN GRAZE. Bring Rod McKuen. And that *overwhelming* dog. (*She steps into the Out Tray and disappears, banker's order in hand.*)

NOBODADDY (*rubbing his hands*). Only one other application. From a chappie called Blake. Rather arrogant letter really. (*Waves letter around in the air.*) Anyone know the feller? William Blake? Anyone heard of him?

SIR JOSHUA. I must confess I've crossed swords with him in the past. So the only decent thing I can do is to stay out of any discussion of his merits.

NOBODADDY. But we've got to ask someone who knows about him.

KLOPSTOCK. What about Robert Southey? Sound chap, Southey.

LADY TWAT. Southey? Not the bolshy? Didn't he write a play about that medieval guerrilla?

KLOPSTOCK. You mean Wat Tyler. Yes, but Southey was young then. Since that time he's published a series in *Encounter* about why he left the party and he's had his teeth fashioned into small but perfect likenesses of Our Gracious Majesty.

(*All* COMMITTEE *stand for a second and then sit down again.*) Haven't you, Bob?

(SOUTHEY *enters, wearing dark glasses, one shirtsleeve rolled up. He pockets a syringe and rolls down his sleeve as he speaks.*)

SOUTHEY. When I saw Blake, his strange designs for his own compositions in verse were not ready for sale, nor did I ever hear that they were so. Much as he is to be admired, he was at the time so evidently insane, that the predominant feeling in conversing with him, or even looking at him, could only be sorrow and compassion. I came away from the visit with so sad a feeling that I never repeated it. You could not have delighted in him, his madness was too evident, too fearful.

(*Smiling, he pulls back the lapel of his jacket to show a silver star.*)

NOBODADDY. Thanks a lot, Bob.

SOUTHEY (*exiting*). Bang, bang, William Blake, I'm dead.

NOBODADDY. Knew his mother. Wonderful woman.

LADY TWAT. I'd be intrigued to see this Blake. Just for fun.

NOBODADDY. Surely it's settled. Southey doesn't like him, and Southey liked Lord Nelson.

KLOPSTOCK. Just for the record, we should see Blake. Besides, he's been waiting outside for (*looks at his watch*) forty-five years. Mr Blake, would you care to join us?

(BLAKE *steps out of the In Tray and on to the table.*)

BLAKE. I've come for my money.

LADY TWAT. It's not quite as simple as that, Mr Cock.

SIR JOSHUA. Our grants are reserved for specific artistic projects.

BLAKE. I'm working on a project. With my brothers and sisters. Building.

NOBODADDY. Building? Building? Not quite our line of country.

BLAKE. We are building Jerusalem. In England.

KLOPSTOCK. We expect our artists to sing for their supper.

NOBODADDY. Perhaps you'd like to explain yourself with a curriculum vitae, references from your local Archbishop and undertaker and a full frontal nude photograph of your soul?

BLAKE. I'll read a poem. (*He takes a crumpled piece of paper out of his pocket, unfolds it and begins to read aloud, not rhetorically, but as if laying down building instructions.*)

What are those golden builders doing?...

Is that Calvary and Golgotha

Becoming a building of pity and compassion? ...

(BLAKE *sees that the B.C.C. members are grinning, winking, settling down for a snooze, etc. So he walks down the table, sits on the end of it and reads directly to the audience. B.C.C. freeze.*)

... a building of pity and compassion? Lo!

The stones are pity, and the bricks, well wrought affections

Enamel'd with love & kindness, & the tiles engraven gold,

Labour of merciful hands: the beams & rafters are forgiveness:

The mortar & cement of the work, tears of honesty: the nails

And the screws & iron braces are well wrought blandishments

And well contrived words, firm fixing, never forgotten,

Always comforting the remembrance: the floors,
    humility:
The ceilings, devotion: the hearths, thanksgiving.
Prepare the furniture, O Lambeth, in thy pitying looms,
The curtains, woven tears & sighs wrought into lovely
    forms
For comfort; there the secret furniture of Jerusalem's
    chamber
Is wrought. Lambeth! the Bride, the Lamb's Wife,
    loveth thee.
Thou art one with her & knowest not of self in thy
    supreme joy.
Go on, builders in hope!

(KLOPSTOCK *has unfrozen and is urging* BLAKE *away.*)

KLOPSTOCK (*coughing*). Thank you Mr Blake. We'll let you
know.

BLAKE (*looking round, summing up the B.C.C.'s reaction, turning
back to the audience and jerking his thumb at the Committee as
he exits quickly*). These are the destroyers of Jerusalem!

KLOPSTOCK. It seems quite obvious that Mr Blake does not
understand the mechanics of success.

SIR JOSHUA. He does tend to bite the hand which has no intention of feeding him.

LADY TWAT. There's one thing worse than dumb insolence –
eloquent insolence.

KLOPSTOCK. Rather destructive, rather destructive.

NOBODADDY. Ought to keep tabs on a chappie like that. Think
I know just the feller for the job.

(NOBODADDY *presses buzzer.* SCOFIELD *appears from the
In Tray with a large kit-bag.*)

SCOFIELD. Sergeant Scofield, my lord, recently seconded to
the Media Police.

NOBODADDY. The problem, Sergeant, is William Blake.

SCOFIELD. Ah … Blake. (*Pause*) No problem, sir. I've designed a personalized mantrap for that gent, I'll demonstrate it if you could help me change into a civilian disguise while I give voice to a most potent song of aggression.

NOBODADDY. Josh! Klopstock! You know what your valets do? Do it to the Sergeant!

(SIR JOSHUA *and* KLOPSTOCK *unpack* SCOFIELD's *kit-bag. While he sings, they take off his uniform and dress him in a somewhat dated spivvy outfit – electric-blue zoot suit, with long drape, wide trousers, Mickey Mouse shoes. Wide hat. Black shirt. Arthur English tie. Dark glasses. Harlem, 1943, is the idea.*)

SCOFIELD (*sings, as a malevolent incantation*).

I was angry with my friend:
I told my wrath, my wrath did end.
I was angry with my foe:
I told it not, my wrath did grow.

And I water'd it in fears,
Night & morning with my tears;
And I sunned it with smiles,
And with soft deceitful wiles.

And it grew both day and night,
Till it bore an apple bright;
And my foe beheld it shine,
And he knew that it was mine,

And into my garden stole
When the night had veil'd the pole:
In the morning glad I see
My foe outstretch'd beneath the tree.

(*He is now dressed. He selects a cosh from his kitbag.*)

You are about to witness a demonstration of the art of Blake-bovvering. Now what's the enemy's most vulnerable point? That's right – compassion. He's what we in the

Sergeant's Mess call an under-dog fancier. I intend to hammer him down into the ground with his own weakness for weaklings. And I'd be grateful if you could have the scene changed to a supermarket, including the alleged Blake. Thank you.

(*Scene changes to a supermarket with Muzak drifting in the air and shoppers with wire carts on wheels sleepwalking up and down between shelves laden with tinned goods. Cash registers bash away intermittently.* SCOFIELD *wheels in a* MECHANICAL CREATURE *in a wire cart. The* MECHANICAL CREATURE *is an ambiguous animal which moves on wheels, but it's hard to tell whether it's an animal or a machine, or a plant for that matter, as fronds grow from its head. It is, primarily, a piece of property. When hit, it emits sounds of despair, which should not be the sounds of one identifiable animal, but a mixture of sounds of animals, humans, wood, water and metal under pressure.* SCOFIELD *has this* CREATURE *on a lead.* SCOFIELD *takes on a perky, Max Millerish personality during the following scene.*

SCOFIELD *waits and watches.* BLAKE *enters one aisle with wire cart, puts a couple of big cans marked* 'Milton' *in his cart. Simultaneously,* SIR JOSHUA *comes down a parallel aisle, filling his cart with anything within reach. At the end of the aisle,* SIR JOSHUA *and* BLAKE *are face to face as their carts collide.*)

BLAKE. Sir Joshua ... I understand I'm not getting a grant.

SIR JOSHUA. I don't think we've met ...

(BLAKE *picks up* SIR JOSHUA *and dumps him in* SIR JOSHUA's *own wire cart.*)

SIR JOSHUA (*in a great panic*). Aren't you William Blake the supreme genius? I'm Sir Joshua Rat's twin brother, Sir Joshua from the Old Folks at Home Home for Old Folk and can I say what a great innocence and experience it is to meet a thunderbolt from the blues like you and what I always say is – GAARAAPH!!!

(BLAKE *has given the shopping cart bearing* SIR JOSHUA *a huge push and it scoots off the far side of the stage. Great sound of collapsing tins from off stage.*)

BLAKE. If you can't beat 'em, fuck 'em.

(BLAKE *resumes his shopping.* SCOFIELD *spots his moment and begins to belabour his* CREATURE *with his cosh. The* CREATURE *howls.*)

SCOFIELD. You five-legged pair of imported ex-officer's combinations. You wall-arsed daughter of a polystyrene sofa. Get up there.

(SCOFIELD *hits the* CREATURE *again.* BLAKE *leaves his shopping and comes round in a fury.*)

BLAKE. Hit that creature once again, and I'll break your truncheon over your trousers.

SCOFIELD (*with cool, simulated anger*). Now hang on, brother, hang on. You're about to indulge in a classic case of interference between a man and his private property. You know how that game always ends.

BLAKE. In tears?

SCOFIELD. In chains.

BLAKE. What is that poor creature?

SCOFIELD. Mine.

BLAKE. But *what* is it?

SCOFIELD (*bashing it to emphasize the point*). Mine, Mine, Mine.

(BLAKE *suddenly grabs the cosh.*)

I see. That changes the situation slightly. (*Pats the creature.*) There's a good thing.

BLAKE. I know *whose* you say it is. But *what* is it?

SCOFIELD. It's just property. *My* property.

(SCOFIELD *presses a button, or pulls a lever and the* CREATURE's *jaws open.* SCOFIELD *picks an apple from the shelves and tosses it into the* CREATURE's *mouth. The jaws close, and the* CREATURE *emits glad noises.*)

Good property, there's a pretty piece of property.

BLAKE. Is it really alive?

SCOFIELD. Not in the sense that I'm alive.

BLAKE. Is it mechanical? Clockwork, perhaps?

SCOFIELD. No, I wouldn't call it a machine.

BLAKE. I thought I caught the smell of life from it.

SCOFIELD. Oh, *life*. There's a sort of life in it. More life than a parsnip, I'd say, livelier than a wurzel. But rather less kick than a spring onion. Somewhere about your beetroot level of evolution, I'd reckon.

BLAKE. It doesn't look like a beetroot to me.

SCOFIELD. Who called it a beetroot? Don't start awarding your fancy titles to my property. I know what you're after. I can tell. London's jam-packed with Y-Front Willies and Jockstrap Johnnies like you, steaming round Golden Square after a bit of blubber. Go on, admit it, you fancy it, don't you? Go on. Everyone does. (*To Audience*) You wouldn't mind a bit now, would you? There you are. And you wouldn't mind a bash at it either, would you? There's no need to be ashamed, you're human, I'll give you that, you're a man I'd say by the cut of your jib, and whenever a real man sees a bit of private property, well, the message slams him in the private parts and that little kettle in his belly begins to steam and whistle.

BLAKE. I like it. I pity it anyway. But that doesn't mean I want it.

SCOFIELD. Pull the other one, it plays the 1812 Overture. (*To* CREATURE) Says he doesn't want you.

(CREATURE *moans*.)

BLAKE. I'm interested in it. I like looking at it. But I don't want to own it. Why should I?

SCOFIELD. Don't you know, you morbid voyeur? Where've you been since 1757? Property. Don't you know why you really, deep down inside yourself, want it just as much as everyone else? So you can do what you like with it whenever

you want to, and when it's got the dry-rot or there's a groan
in its gear-box or the string round its handle is impregnated
with old cold sweat or there's a hairline crack on its rim full
of bacteria – why then, you flog it. (*Changing gear suddenly.*)
Didn't we meet in the Forsyte Saga?

BLAKE. Are you tired of it? Is that why you hit it?

SCHOFIELD. Tired of it? Why should I be tired of it? I built it
up from a single tobacconist and undertaker's lock-up into
a chain of chainstores selling chains. Look, before I married
it, it was a bottomless waitress in a cafeteria frequented by
Scandinavian stokers. When it passed into my possession,
the Tate Gallery thought it was a fake Salvador Dali by
Salvador Dali. And look at it today. A cynosure, sir, an
unmitigated cynosure.

BLAKE. But how did you get hold of it?

SCOFIELD. I was asked to look after it by a bloke I met in a pub.
He told me it fell off the back of a lorry. It fell to pieces in my
head. I stuck it together and that gives me rights. Proper
property rights. You want to look up your Magna Carta,
my friend, you want to find out which side your brother's
buttered on. You'll have to get up early in the evening if you
want to get hold of a sweet little hullabaloo like this.

(CROWD *has been gathering around, mainly well-dressed*
gents. They bring with them a rostrum, to which SCOFIELD
gradually moves during the next few speeches.)

BLAKE. I don't want it, but I'd buy it off you if I could afford it.

SCOFIELD. There you go, you are human. You are after a little
bit of object, aren't you? You're not above a touch of the old
possessions, eh?

BLAKE. I'd like to buy it just to stop you bashing it around.

SCOFIELD. Now, now, don't let's get holy. You'd bash it if you
had it, you know. Bash, bash, pretty bash, you'd go,
wouldn't you?

BLAKE. No, I'd give it its freedom.

SCOFIELD. Come on, sir. No need to bash about the bush. I can see you're in the trade by the way you hold yourself. I can tell you're a dealer by the spread of your wingspan. How about slipping me a slimline cheque for it before the auction starts?

BLAKE (*being pushed to one side by* CROWD *as* SCOFIELD *mounts the rostrum*). How much will you let it go for?

SCOFIELD (*leaning from rostrum, intimately*). Everything you have.

(BLAKE *stares at him unhappily. Dead pause.*)

SCOFIELD (*publicly and noisily*). All right, ladies and gentlemen, here it is, Exhibit A, Lot One, the only lot. In fact you might say the whole bloody lot, because that's what it's got. I've got the pride and peacock to be selling this exhilarating piece of private property, you've all got your sales catalogues, tattoo guidebooks and bloodstock encyclopaedias at the ready, so hold on to your knickers and here we go. Mr Blake, would you mind stepping up to the rostrum? We can't start the auction without *you*.

(BLAKE *is pulled into and surrounded by the* CROWD, *who grab the cosh from him and pass it up to* SCOFIELD. SCOFIELD *beats three times on the rostrum with the cosh. As he begins his spiel, people in the* CROWD *begin to bid by raising legs, whirling their heads around in circles, baring their teeth, etc. During the auction they hum with almost closed mouths, an increasingly loud, wordless chorus of excitement. The effect of the individual bids should be that of one person doing a single-movement, quirky dance, while the rest of the* CROWD *freezes.*)

Right. What am I bid, what am I bid? Thank you ... I've got a six-finger exercise. I've got fifty-eight and a half bottles of glue over there. Will the gent in the middle kindly raise his umbrella or lower it, thank you? Lady over there bids two underslung anvils and a snakeskin helmet. Who'll give me a mastodon pasty? Do I hear a mastodon pasty? Thank you sir, you're a saint of the highest water. I'm bid fourteen thousand acres of red gravel in Derbyshire.

ARISTOCRATIC VOICE FROM CROWD. Good old Derbyshire!

SCOFIELD. Fourteen thousand acres of – I'm bid an india-rubber piano, a high fidelity bulldog with his head stuck in a Beatrix Potter chamberpot and a silent movie version of *The Sound of Music*. I'm bid a collection of graffiti from the Great Wall of China and a crocodile egg hatched by President Nixon.

VOICE FROM CROWD. Venceremos!

SCOFIELD. I'm bid a moon-ladder, fifteen pairs of pre-war surgical galactic goloshes and a semi-detached igloo on the Martian Grand Canal. Will the lady in premature mourning please leave herself alone? I am bid a poisoned planet. I am bid a poisoned planet and a lonely sun. I am bid a poisoned planet, a lonely sun and an egg-shaped universe with vacant possession. Going, going, gone – sold to the gentleman with the concealed bazooka.

(SIR JOSHUA RAT, *now dressed as himself, steps out of the crowd with two uniformed* PRISON WARDERS, *who shackle* BLAKE *hand and foot and turn him round to reveal a label on his back saying* LOT ONE. SIR JOSHUA *hands a huge cheque to* SCOFIELD, *who rushes off to cash it, dragging his* CREATURE *behind him.*)

(*exiting*) Try to think of the universe as a game, Mr Blake.

BLAKE. You can't buy me, Sir Joshua.

SIR JOSHUA. That's what they all say at first.

BLAKE. You can't buy anyone.

SIR JOSHUA (*generally*). Slavery is rather pathetic, when you come to think about it. So you don't.

BLAKE (*shouting*). Flesh is not property. I can breathe. You can't

49

buy my breath. My thoughts go on. I am a lamb. It is impossible to own a lamb. I am a tiger –

(CROWD *disperses as* PRISON WARDERS *throw* BLAKE *into a corner on a pile of straw.* BLAKE *is left alone on the stage.*)

I have never been a slave. But I have to learn what it's like to be a slave.

(STEDMAN, *a pleasant-looking tall Englishman, in tropical gear, comes over to* BLAKE. STEDMAN *is sympathetic, up to a point, but very cool and detached. He tends to address the audience rather than* BLAKE.)

STEDMAN. Mr Blake, I'd like to help you –

BLAKE. A good intention –

STEDMAN. I can't get your chains off, of course –

BLAKE. That would be illegal –

STEDMAN. But I might be able to throw a little work your way. Help you buy your freedom.

BLAKE. Anything considered.

STEDMAN. Thing is, I've just come back from five years in Surinam.

BLAKE. What were you doing there?

STEDMAN. Well, my heart wasn't in it.

BLAKE. That's very bad.

STEDMAN. I didn't like it, but it was what I was hired to do. I had to put down a revolt of the slaves.

BLAKE. I knew it was very bad.

STEDMAN. I'm a soldier, you know, a professional.

BLAKE. Very bad.

STEDMAN. Yes, but I didn't know when I signed on. I didn't know how they tortured those poor souls. Only comfort was that it wasn't a British colony. It was bad, though, you're right, especially when they tortured female slaves.

BLAKE. Do women feel more pain?

STEDMAN. Well, it's worse for women.

BLAKE. I expect it is. And you want to hire me?

STEDMAN. You've been highly recommended, Mr Blake.

BLAKE. What do you want me to do?

STEDMAN. You see, I've written a book about my experiences out there –

BLAKE. Oh, you write?

STEDMAN. In a rough sort of way, sir, yes I write. I took a lot of photos while I was there, but they're pretty blurred. I thought you might use them as the basis for a series of engravings. For my book on putting down the slave revolt.

(STEDMAN *takes some photos from his pocket. He hands one to* BLAKE, *who examines it minutely.*)

(*Apologetically*) The damp got into the film. But you get the idea.

BLAKE. I get a great many ideas from it. This is a great man. A man of great dignity.

STEDMAN. Sure you've got the right one? Ah, yes. I call that one – 'Negro hung alive by the ribs to the gallows'. Had a lot of spunk.

BLAKE (*shutting him up*). His eyes are talking to me.

(*Short silence while* BLAKE *examines the photo.*)

STEDMAN. He survived for three days. Here's another. This chap's being broken on the rack. The other black in the background, he's the executioner. His job was to break all our friend's bones one by one.

BLAKE. I will draw and engrave this man with his bones broken.

STEDMAN. He was quite a joker, actually. There was a bit of a crowd. I was on guard, munching a bit of bread. And that chap with the bones shouted out: 'Hey, mister. Look over there and you'll find the hand they chopped off me lying under that berry bush.' I said to him: 'I have no use for your hand.' To which he replied: 'But you've got some bread, haven't you? Well, it's shameful that a white man should eat dry bread. Get under that bush, grab my hand and make yourself a sandwich.'

BLAKE (*looking at another photo*). Is this you?

STEDMAN. Yes, that's me, with a rebel Negro prostrate at my feet. ''Twas theirs to fall, but mine to feel the wound.'

BLAKE. What?

STEDMAN (*embarrassed*). You know – ''Twas theirs to fall, but mine to feel the wound.' Quotation.

BLAKE. Yes. You didn't actually feel the wounds then?

STEDMAN. Course not. It's a metaphor. You know what a metaphor is, don't you?

BLAKE. I know what a fucking wound is.

    (*Silence.* STEDMAN *begins to take his photos back but* BLAKE *grabs another.*)

And what do you call this one?

STEDMAN. Actually, it's called 'A Contented Slave'.

BLAKE. Yes, he looks … What are those letters on his arm?

STEDMAN. He's branded with his owner's initials. They have to be branded, you know, legally.

BLAKE. J. G. S.?

STEDMAN. That's me. J. G. Stedman. He was one of mine. (*Taking back last photo.*) Well, Mr Blake, I'm sorry you feel as you do. I'm sure your feelings do you credit even if they do no good. I'll take my little problem elsewhere.

    (BLAKE *grabs* STEDMAN's *wrist till he is forced to drop the photos.*)

BLAKE. You misunderstand me, Mr Stedman. I'll engrave your designs. I'll do better. I'll brand them on to the paper.

STEDMAN (*retreating and exiting*). Very well. Kind of you, very kind of you, Mr Blake.

    (BLAKE's *engravings from* A Narrative of a Five Years' Expedition Against the Revolted Negroes of Surinam *by Captain J. G. Stedman are projected. The* CHORUS *form a swaying mass in chains and almost total darkness behind* BLAKE. *As he sings, standing in his chains, they begin to move forward to join him.*)

BLAKE (*sings*).

> Let the slave grinding at the mill run out into the field,
> Let him look up into the heavens & laugh in the bright
> air;
> Let the inchained soul, shut up in darkness and in sighing,
> Whose face has never seen a smile in thirty weary years,
> Rise and look out; his chains are loose, his dungeon doors
> are open;
> And let his wife and children return from the oppressor's
> scourge.
> They look behind at every step & believe it is a dream,
> Singing:

CHORUS (*sing*).

> The Sun has left his blackness, & has found a fresher
> morning,
> And the fair Moon rejoices in the clear & cloudless night;
> For Empire is no more, and now the Lion & Wolf shall
> cease.

BLAKE (*sings*).

> For every thing that lives

CHORUS (*sing*).

> is Holy.

BLAKE (*sings*).

> For every thing that lives

CHORUS (*sing*).

> is Holy.

CHORUS (*sing*).

> For every thing that lives
> is Holy.
>
> (CHORUS *continue with this chant, developing it quietly,
> varying it, while* BLAKE *speaks the following verses over the
> chant, after his chains have been removed.*)

BLAKE (*speaking over chant of* CHORUS).

> What is the price of Experience? Do men buy it for a song?

Or wisdom for a dance in the street? No, it is bought with
 the price
Of all that a man hath, his house, his wife, his children.
Wisdom is sold in the desolate market where none come
 to buy,
And in the wither'd field where the farmer plows for
 bread in vain.

It is an easy thing to triumph in the summer's sun
And in the vintage, & to sing on the waggon loaded with
 corn.
It is an easy thing to talk of patience to the afflicted,
To speak the laws of prudence to the houseless wanderer,
To listen to the hungry raven's cry in wintry season
When the red blood is fill'd with wine & with the marrow
 of lambs.

It is an easy thing to laugh at wrathful elements,
To hear the dog howl at the wintry door, the ox in the
 slaughter house moan;
To see a god on every wind & a blessing on every blast;
To hear sounds of love in the thunder storm that destroys
 our enemies' house;
To rejoice in the blight that covers his field, & the sickness
 that cuts off his children,
While our olive & vine sing & laugh round our door,
 & our children bring fruit & flowers.

Then the groan & the dolor are quite forgotten, & the
 slave grinding at the mill,
And the captive in chains, & the poor in the prison, & the
 soldier in the field
When the shatter'd bone hath laid him groaning among
 the happier dead.
It is an easy thing to rejoice in the tents of prosperity:

Thus would I sing & thus rejoice: but it is not so with me.

BLAKE & CHORUS (*sing*).

For every thing that lives is Holy.
For every thing that lives is Holy.
For every thing that lives is Holy.
For every thing that lives is Holy.

ACT TWO

BLAKE's *workroom.*
KATE *is at work colouring a page.* BLAKE *holds baby.*

BLAKE (*speaks, as if proofreading*).
> Sweet dreams, form a shade
> O'er my lovely infant's head;
> Sweet dreams of pleasant streams
> By happy silent moony beams.
>
> Sweet sleep, with soft down
> Weave thy brows an infant crown.
> Sweet sleep, Angel mild,
> Hover o'er my happy child.
>
> Sweet smiles, in the night,
> Hover over my delight;
> Sweet smiles, Mother's smiles,
> All the livelong night beguiles.
>
> Sweet moans, dovelike sighs,
> Chase not slumber from thy eyes.
> Sweet moans, sweeter smiles,
> All the dovelike moans beguiles.

(*sings*).
> Sleep, sleep, happy child,
> All creation slept and smil'd;
> Sleep, sleep, happy sleep,
> While o'er thee thy mother weep.
>
> Sweet babe, in thy face
> Holy image I can trace.

57

Sweet babe, once like thee,
Thy maker lay and wept for me,

Wept for me, for thee, for all,
When he was an infant small.
Thou his image ever see,
Heavenly face that smiles on thee,

Smiles on thee, on me, on all;
Who became an infant small.
Infant smiles are his own smiles;
Heaven & earth to peace beguiles.

BLAKE. Come on, Kate, we can put him down now. (*Proudly*)
That song *worked*.

(KATE *takes the baby and puts him to bed behind the curtains.*
BLAKE *sits and begins to work.* KATE *joins him.*)

FUSELI (*off*). Knock knock.

BLAKE. Who goes there?

FUSELI (*off*). Henry Fuseli, 1759 to 1832. With Sam Palmer in
tow.

BLAKE. Lurch in.

(FUSELI, *a somewhat rough and shambling artist, lumbers in
followed by a shy young* SAMUEL PALMER, *who worships*
BLAKE. FUSELI *and* BLAKE *embrace, while* PALMER
smiles nervously in the background.)

FUSELI. So you finally made it, Mr Blake?

BLAKE. I make things all the time. What'd I make?

FUSELI. You mean – nobody told you? Nobody phoned?

KATE. Phone's cut off.

FUSELI. The only man on the island who can communicate
over one hundred years and the G.P.O. cuts him off. (*To the
stalls*) You call that civilization, Sir Kenneth?

BLAKE. Wasn't like that. I was trying to finish this book. (*Picks
up a huge golden volume.*)

FUSELI. What's that? *The Thoughts of William Blake*, vest-pocket edition?

PALMER. That's *Jerusalem*.

KATE. He's been working on it for fourteen years.

BLAKE. I was just engraving the final plate – 'The Builders of Jerusalem'. And the phone rang. So I picked up the scissors and cut the wire.

FUSELI. You always were a fool for symbolism, Blake. Look what you've missed. (*Produces magazine.*) *Melody Maker*, page two, L.P. charts. Number One – 'The Marriage of Heaven and Hell', by William Blake.

PALMER. That's not all. Everybody's writing books about you.

FUSELI. They're bidding for your laundry bills at Sotheby's.

PALMER. They're lecturing about you.

FUSELI. That's right. The professors are asking: Was Blake mad? Was Blake impotent? Was Blake the Duke of Wellington?

PALMER. You can buy Blake T-shirts.

FUSELI. Blake mugs.

PALMER. Blake wallpaper.

FUSELI. Blake mascara.

KATE. What?

PALMER. Mascara. (*Shrugging lugubriously.*) Supposed to give your eyes that visionary gleam.

BLAKE (*to himself, puzzled*). Mascara.

FUSELI. I tell you, it's a Blake bonanza.

BLAKE. It's a bit late, innit? I've been dead for more than a hundred years.

FUSELI. Hey, I keep forgetting. Did you have a good death?

BLAKE. Can't remember exactly. Kate, love, what was it like when I died?

(FUSELI *sits on the floor to listen.* PALMER *leans against the wall.* KATE *smiles, remembering one of the good times. Everyone is very relaxed.*)

KATE. Well, you were sixty-nine. You'd been ill for months. You'd finished 'The Last Judgment'. And it was a summer evening.

BLAKE. Yes. I was in bed. And I was drawing you. I said something like: Stay Kate, keep just as you are, I will draw your portrait, for you have ever been an angel to me.

KATE. But it wasn't much like me. It *was* lovely.

BLAKE (*indignantly*). It was a good likeness. (*Shuffles through sheaf of drawings, passes one to* PALMER.) Look, Sam.

(PALMER *looks at the drawing, smiles and nods.*)

PALMER. It's beautiful.

FUSELI. Bit frenzied.

BLAKE. You're a fine one to talk. There wasn't much time.

KATE. And then you were making up hymns and singing them, very quietly into my ear. And I said I liked your songs. And you said: My beloved, they are not mine – no – they are not mine.

PALMER. Did anyone write them down?

BLAKE. No. They were just for Kate.

FUSELI. That's a pretty sensible death, Blake.

BLAKE. It's good you dropped in today. It's my birthday. Sit down here and you shall see a procession of great poets pass through our workroom, to pay their annual tributes. Here comes Geoffrey now.

(BLAKE, KATE, FUSELI *and* PALMER *sit down.*

CHAUCER, *dressed for hiking, knapsack, stick, hearty, comes in.* BLAKE *shakes hands with him.*)

CHAUCER (*sings*).

Chaucer's the name,
Number one on your poetry list,
Gentlemanly joker,
Medieval behaviourist.
My real name's Geoffrey,
But they call me Dan,

And it's good to see you,
Always glad to meet a fan.
(KATE *pours* CHAUCER *a drink from a jug. He grins and swigs.*
SHAKESPEARE *enters dressed as a cowboy.*)

SHAKESPEARE (*sings*).

I'm Willy Shakespeare
(KATE *gives him a drink hurriedly, curtsying.*)
Thank you ma'am,
I just rode in on Pegasus and I don't give a damn
For any pen-slinger who thinks he can out-write me
'Cos I'm the greatest gun in the terror territory.
You never saw such shooting,
I can drop 'em with one line –
(CHAUCER *reaches into his wind-cheater for a gun, but* SHAKESPEARE *outdraws him.*)
(*Sings staccato as he fires both guns.*)
The multitudinous seas incarnadine.
(CHAUCER *pretends to be shot, then smiles, goes over and shakes* SHAKESPEARE'S *hand.*)

CHAUCER. All right, you're boss. Have a drink, relax. Meet
Billy Blake.
(SHAKESPEARE *eyes* BLAKE, *moves towards him, extends his hand.*)

SHAKESPEARE. You stick to poetry, pardner. Ain't no theatre
big enough for both of us.

KATE. He called you pardner!

BLAKE. Glad to meet you, Mr Shakespeare. Your work's very
important to me.
(SHAKESPEARE *is slightly foxed by this, imagines there may be a hidden insult in it, then realizes there isn't.*)

SHAKESPEARE. Uh … yup.
(SHAKESPEARE *relaxes. Sits by* CHAUCER.)

Yup. (*To* CHAUCER) You got that – the multitudinous seas incarnadine?

CHAUCER. Pretty good. Hey, there's Johnny Milton.

(MILTON, *in track suit, runs to centre of stage.*)

MILTON (*somewhat out of breath, sings*).

A hundred lines before breakfast,
That's the way to keep in trim;
But those lines had better be lofty
Or you're going to end up like him.

(MILTON *points to an indignant* CHAUCER.)

I'm not saying my work's perfect,
Well, I made the odd mistake;
But if there's one man can put it right,
It's you, Mr William Blake.

BLAKE. Much obliged. I'll do my best to justify your crazy ways to Man.

MILTON. That's the spirit. (*To* KATE) No thanks, just a lemonade for me, got to keep my head clear.

SHAKESPEARE. When Willy Shakespeare drinks, everybody drinks.

MILTON. So be it, Will. Lemonade shandy, then.

SHAKESPEARE (*relaxing*). Huh!

BLAKE. And now, ladies and gentlemen, I'd like you to meet the heaviest of all the super-groups – The Romantic Revival! Willy Wordsworth on drums. Percy Bysshe Shelley – bass guitar. Samuel Taylor Coleridge. John Keats. And the singer – you've guessed it, star of sex, screen and Missolonghi – Bad Lord Byron!

(*Group appear as they are named.* KEATS *and* COLERIDGE *harmonize behind* BYRON'*s vocal*).

BYRON (*sings*).

When he was alive everybody used to put him down.
Now they're writing volumes and they say they're sad he's not around.

62

But they wouldn't know Blake if they saw him
And heard him
And shook him by the hand.
They wouldn't know Blake if they took him
And tried him
And shot him from the witness stand.

For Blake was a man like any other man
But he trained his hands to see
And he trained his tongue to pop out of his ears
And he cried with his toenails
And the hairs in his nostrils
Danced to the music of the oxygen.

And they took a thousand million bricks
And they laid down Blake like a foundation stone
And they built a city-prison on his chest
But nothing could hold him down.

For he took a draught of explosive air
And he shook off London like a crust.
And he sang as he stood on the edge of the world
And he worked as he stood as he sang
And he built Jerusalem
He built Jerusalem
With his soft hard
Hard soft hands.

So it's happy birthday William Blake
What you've done can never be undone.
Happy birthday William Blake
Tyger of Jerusalem and Lamb of London.
Happy birthday happy birthday
Happy birthday William Blake.

COLERIDGE (*slightly high, but serious*). Had a dream last night.

Was sitting at a table with dozens of television men in suits.
They were all talking about moneyandart, moneyandart,
you know. Then I saw Dylan Thomas the other end of the
table, all crumpled up and sad. So I said: 'The trouble with
England is, poets are treated like shit.' And Dylan looked up
and he shook his head and he grinned at me and he said: 'No.
The trouble with England is, *most* people are treated like
shit.'

FUSELI. Watch your language. Here come the Late Victorians!
> (*Enter, dressed in striped blazers, boaters and white flannels, a
> barbershop quintet of poets –* KIPLING, TENNYSON,
> BROWNING, WHITMAN *and* EDWARD LEAR. TEN-
> NYSON *is the dignified bass.* BROWNING, *the ladykiller, has
> the next lowest voice.* WHITMAN *the next highest voice.*
> LEAR *high tenor, but should be a very beautiful voice, though
> the others treat him with some contempt.* KIPLING, *although
> tall and military in bearing, sings falsetto with the air of a man
> doing his duty.*
>
> *They all move with great precision, and there should be some
> very full barbershop chords. As they announce themselves they
> raise their boaters and place them on their hearts – there should
> be plenty of this sort of thing.*)

TENNYSON (*sings*).
> Alfred Lord Tennyson.

BROWNING (*sings*).
> Robert Browning.

WHITMAN (*sings*).
> Walt Whitman.

LEAR (*sings*).
> Edward Lear, I'm afraid.

KIPLING (*sings*).
> Rudyard Kipling, Defender of the Faith.

QUINTET (*sings*).
> We've come in an advisory capacity

To instruct you in the art of poesy
We live on Parnassus, it's a beautiful view,
Just follow in our footsteps and you'll join us too-oo-
    oo-oo
If you can

WHITMAN (*sings*).
    Skate on your toe-nails from here to the Aleutians
    And be back in time for Armageddon.

QUINTET (*sings*).
    If you can.

BROWNING (*sings*).
    Run a dozen separate revolutions
    And emerge with your beautiful head on.

QUINTET (*sings*).
    If you can

KIPLING (*sings*).
    Turn constipation
    Into a song.

QUINTET (*sings*).
    If you can

TENNYSON (*sings*).
    Screw Euston Station
    Till it chimes like a gong

LEAR (*sings*).
    And carve your verse on granite
    With your luminous dong.

QUINTET (*sings*).
    If you can do all this although you're feathered and tarred
    If you can keep your arrows of desire hard
    If you can live on biscuits and a union card

KIPLING (*sings*).
    You'll be a man,

WHITMAN (*sings*).
    You'll be a world,

BROWNING (*sings*).

    You'll be a planet,

TENNYSON (*sings*).

    You'll be a bard!

QUINTET (*sings*).

    So sing it right

    And get your cash on the night

    And onward!

    Upward!

    You're bound to be famous.

    Right on!

    Avanti!

    Venceremos!

WHITMAN (*sings*).

    For the poet is the man who runs a brothel at a loss.

LEAR (*sings*).

    He shares his Christmas pudding with Jesus on the cross.

KIPLING (*sings*).

    If he kneels for a knighthood, just for a laugh

TENNYSON (*sings*).

    The Queen swings her sword back and chops him in half.

QUINTET (*sings*).

    So sing it right

    And get your cash on the night

    Onward!

    Upward!

    Wise ignoramus

    Right on!

    Avanti!

    And venceremos!

    And happy birthday William Blake.

BLAKE. Cheers – help yourselves. (*Indicating drink.*) But is that the lot? I wouldn't mind seeing Allen.

SHAKESPEARE (*clicks his fingers*). Ginsberg. Hey, Ginsberg, get
up here!

(ALLEN GINSBERG *enters, true to life as possible, not a
caricature.*

GINSBERG *stands immediately in front of* BLAKE. *They
stare at each other. Then, simultaneously, they embrace each
other.*

THE ROMANTIC REVIVAL *take up their instruments.*

The other poets, including BLAKE, *group round microphones.*)

POETS (*sing*).

    Poetry

    Glues your soul together

    Poetry

    Wears dynamite shoes

    Poetry

    Is the spittle on the mirror

    Poetry

    Wears nothing but the blues.

CHAUCER (*sings*).

    It's the mongoloid gargoyle that falls off the cathedral

    To land on the crown of the Queen.

SHAKESPEARE (*sings*).

    Grab it while you can, it's the magical needle

    It's bitter sixteen and its flesh is bright green.

POETS (*sing*).

    Poetry

    Glues your soul together

    Poetry

    Wears dynamite shoes

    Poetry

    Is the spittle on the mirror

    Poetry

    Wears nothing but the blues.

MILTON (*sings*).

Nixon hasn't got it, but there's plenty in Fidel,
Slap your sherry trifle on my sewing-machine.

BYRON (*sings*).

Bend it into bowlines but you'll never break it

GINSBERG (*sings*).

The only way to make it is the way you make it

BLAKE (*sings*).

Only thing that matters is the way you shake it.

POETS (*sing*).

Poetry

Glues your soul together

Poetry

Wears dynamite shoes

Poetry

Is the spittle on the mirror

KATE (*sings*).

Poetry

Wears nothing but the blues.

(*By now all the poets have drinks and are refilling each other's
glasses, knocking it back, and it's turning into a party.*)

KEATS. O for a beaker full of the warm South,
With buddled beadles winking at the brim –

SHAKESPEARE. Johnny Keats, Johnny Keats, over here.

KEATS. What's up, guv?

SHAKESPEARE. Listen, pretty boy – you may be the kid with
the curls, but who's got the biggest critical response around
here?

BYRON. You wanna know what critics think, you gotta ask the
critics.

WHITMAN. Bring on the critics!

(*The* CHORUS OF CRITICS *come charging on. They are all
girls wearing erotic variations on military uniforms and wielding
various weapons. They emerge as a ferocious, high-disciplined
chorus line, high kicks and all.*)

CRITICS (*sing*).

> The penetrating analysis
> And implicit reference
> To mature standards and interests
> Is pretty disassociating!
>
> (CRITICS *repeat this snappy Leavisian chorus once or twice, but are broken up by* COLERIDGE *staggering through the ranks. They stop and stare at him.*)

COLERIDGE. Hello, critics. Got any O?

LEADING CRITIC. Got any what, Mr Coleridge?

COLERIDGE. You know – O, the Big O? Chinese toffee? Xanadu Zoom Zoom? Ancient Mariner Black Shag? You know, Opium.

CRITICS (*in unison*). What kind of critics do you take us for?

BYRON. The way you write, sounds like you high all the time.

KEATS. Gang of bloody scrubbers, I'd say.

LEADING CRITIC. Scrubber yourself, John Keats. Having it off with nightingales. And Grecian Urns.

CHAUCER. Right, that does it. That's enough of your metaphysical agro.

> (POETS *plus* FUSELI *and* PALMER *and* CRITICS *pile into each other. Slapstick fight ensues, until finally every poet except* WHITMAN *and* GINSBERG *has lifted a* CRITIC *off the stage and carried her off with howls of lust.*
>
> BLAKE *and* KATE *are by now back at work.* WHITMAN *and* GINSBERG *look at each other.*)

WHITMAN, One thing I've learned, Mr Ginsberg. Those English poets grab it wherever they can.

GINSBERG. The lineaments of gratified desire, Mr Whitman.

> (WHITMAN *picks* GINSBERG *up in his arms and rushes off stage.*)

KATE. At least the Brontë sisters would have helped clear up.

BLAKE. Well, it's only once a year.

> (SCOFIELD *appears from behind the door.*)

SCOFIELD (*somewhat drunk*). Remember me, Blake – Second Lieutenant Scofield. Just dropped in to see what you're up to.

BLAKE. You can just drop out again.

SCOFIELD. Come, come, Mr Blake. I'm a soldier of the Queen and I'm here on behalf of the people of England to nose around.

BLAKE. The people of England are like a parcel of children. When the revolution comes it will overwhelm Europe in an hour and when it comes to English ground, every Englishman will have his choice whether to get out or join the revolution. Damn the Queen of England. All her soldiers are slaves.

KATE. And so are all her poor people.

(*Bedroom curtains part to reveal a* JUDGE. *A defence* LAWYER *rushes into the room.*)

LAWYER. I am instructed by Mr Blake to deny every pernicious word which the soldier Scofield alleges that he uttered. Mr Blake is as loyal a subject as any man here. He feels as much indignation at the idea of exposing to contempt or injury the sacred person of his sovereign as any man. Do we not hear every day from the mouths of thousands in the streets the exclamation of God Save the Queen?

JUDGE. Certainly we do.

BLAKE. Which postal district do you live in?

LAWYER. There is no doubt that the crime which is laid to the charge of my client, Mr Blake, is a crime of the most extraordinary malignity.

JUDGE. Prisoner at the bar, what is your occupation?

BLAKE. The building of Jerusalem.

SCOFIELD. If you'll only read this book, your honour. It's called *Jerusalem* and –

JUDGE. No thank you, I don't read. Blake, the charge against you is very grave. Sedition, a hanging matter. How do you intend to repulse that charge?

BLAKE. It's my business to survive. So I swear that this is what I said to Scofield: It is the duty of every counter-revolutionary to make the counter-revolution. God bless the Queen of England. All her soldiers are free.

KATE. And so are all her poor people.

BLAKE. To put it bluntly, I shall lie to you, and I will tell good lies, and you will believe me.

JUDGE. I'm impressed by your frankness. Flabbergasted. In fact, Mr Blake, you have blown my mind. Let me give my ruling. I rule that the human body is not guilty. I rule that society is out of order and the times are out of joint.

(*Exit* LAWYER *and* JUDGE.)

SCOFIELD. But he *did* say God Damn the Queen. A direct reference to Good Queen Anne the Dead. You haven't heard the last of this, Mr Blake. I'm going to take it right to the top.

(SCOFIELD *grabs* BLAKE'*s copy of* Jerusalem, *draws a knife and retreats through bedroom curtains.* KATE *restrains* BLAKE. *When* BLAKE *draws curtains* SCOFIELD *has vanished.*)

BLAKE. They keep interrupting my life.

KATE. They might have hung you.

BLAKE. They might have. If they'd bothered to read my poems.

(BLAKE'*s workroom is taken out. Scene changes to* SIR JOSHUA'*s studio.* SIR JOSHUA *enters, flourishing a letter with an impressive heading.*)

SIR JOSHUA. By appointment to His Majesty. By appointment to His Majesty. That'll look good on the bidet. By appointment to His Majesty. If only Andy Warhol were alive to see this.

(*Enter, on a horse,* MAD KING GEORGE THE FIFTY.)

MAD KING. I am Mad King George the Fifty of England, Limited. And it's not much fun. Opening Parliament when I'd sooner close it and run the whole show myself. Head of the Church of England – might as well be chairman of a tapioca pudding. Shaking hands among other things with members of the Commonwealth without regard for colour, creed or money. Ah, unbuttoned lies the head that wears the crown. But are my subjects grateful? No! They mutter against me. Mutter, mutter, they go. And who's the biggest mutterer of the lot? This blake William Bloke.

SIR JOSHUA. Your Majesty, I am privileged to grovel. (*Grovels.*)

MAD KING. An excellent grovel, Sir Joshua. I'm glad you're glad to grovel. They usually are, because of my skill.

SIR JOSHUA (*photographing* MAD KING). What is your skill, Mad King George the Fifty?

MAD KING. I am extremely skilled at hitting children. In fact, I rarely miss.

SIR JOSHUA. Well, how about that one, pop-pickers?

MAD KING. Don't burble, man. If you do so, I shall seek out your children and hit them.

SIR JOSHUA. Probably, like most abuses, it's less than it seems.

MAD KING. You have to hit them more than it seems.

SIR JOSHUA. Any particular children, Your Mad Majesty?

MAD KING. I start at the top and let the rest of the country work downwards. Most mornings I spend hitting the heir to the throne.

SIR JOSHUA. You mean Good King Edward the Horse?

MAD KING. Bash around the brainbox, bash around the brainbox, keeps 'em moving. And I don't play favourites. Good King George the Girl gets his share.

SIR JOSHUA. A good start. But where will it all lead?

MAD KING. Wider still and wider.

SIR JOSHUA. Then why don't I see children being hit everywhere I go?

MAD KING. Because it's more fun in the hall when the front door's shut. I never saw a child who wasn't all the better for two hours in a dark cupboard waiting to be hit. Made me what I am today.

SIR JOSHUA. Your Majestical, I do realize that, in the art of hitting children, the English hold several world records. But what's that got to do with Public Enemy Number One? I mean, what's the connection between William Blake and baby-bashing?

MAD KING. If you have to ask, you'll never know.

SIR JOSHUA. Mad Sire, you have just given me the idea for a masterpiece.

MAD KING. Masterstrokes, that's what the country needs. You don't have to hit them all the time, you know.

SIR JOSHUA. That would be too fatiguing.

MAD KING. You just have to let them know they may be hit at any time. Sometimes you can tell them – it's best to be perfectly frank with children of all ages – you can simply say to them, You are going to be hit. Some time. In three hours, maybe. Or tomorrow. Or two years before retirement. You – are – going – to – be – hit. The thing is to keep them in a state where they expect they're going to be hit. Because then they walk about all funny, like this. (*Walks about in a cowering position.*)

SIR JOSHUA. That's a fine pose, Your Maniac, let me get it down.

(SIR JOSHUA *with camera follows* MAD KING *around as he stumps about in his cowering posture.*)

MAD KING (*still posing*). Of course, the only danger is that one day one's children might grow up and hit one back. But by the time they do that I shall have knocked the nonsense out of their leaky heads. I think I will go to Egypt for my holidays in 1944. I like being in Egypt in 1944 because wherever you walk you're followed by beggar children and you can hit them as much as you like. And kick their parents, if you can call them parents.

73

SIR JOSHUA (*excited*). Your Magistrate, when are we going to have World War One?

MAD KING. You're a turdbrain, Gainsborough, a shitfish.

SIR JOSHUA. I'd rather you called me Sir Joshua. Or Raphael, for that matter.

MAD KING. We've already had World War One, and World War Two if it comes to that. We are now in the process of following up those prototypes. World War Three will be a combination of the most spectacular features of One and Two, plus nine secret new ingredients. And, what is more, it will be available to all.

SIR JOSHUA. He walked with kings yet kept the royal touch. Is there any money in World War Three?

MAD KING. We shall need some World War Three War Artists. Are you any good at painting landscapes which look as if a volcano had vomited all over them? Horizon to horizon? Hot scarlet lava, that's the ticket. And then it turns into a cold thick grey crust of cold hard lava. Are you the right man for the job?

SIR JOSHUA. I could put some figures of children being hit by adults in the corners of the landscape.

MAD KING. Be reasonable. They wouldn't really be alive, would they? But you could have some grownups a bit like statues, covered with that lava stuff but still standing up, petrified in attitudes which make it plain that they were just about to hit their children when the lava got them. The children would have to be petrified too, like Peter Pan in Kensington Gardens.

SIR JOSHUA. Do you miss the Black Death?

MAD KING. No, I am very rich. But there is one thing troubles me in my amalgamated empire. There is a child-man in our midst who must shortly be extinguished.

SIR JOSHUA. I'm not a child-man, sire. If I were, I'd have to hit myself.

MAD KING. You're no child-man. You're the oldest man in the world. Allow me to knight you for that.

SIR JOSHUA. I've been knighted already.

MAD KING. It won't hurt. (*Dubs* SIR JOSHUA.) Arise, arise, Sir Sir Joshua Joshua, and quickly step aside. There's treachery underfoot. This groaning, pleasant land of ours is being taken over by an alien force. More and more people are reading Blake. More and more people are thinking like Blake. They're even beginning to look like Blake, and they all look alike to me. We must stamp out this new race of revolutionary, visionary, pink niggers. You are about to hear an historic speech about the menace of the Blake people from the hitherto comparatively musclebound lips of Mad King George the Fifty. (*Sings ominously.*)

> Evils ... obstacles ... onset of doubt ...
> Troubles ... indisputable and pressing ...
> Troubles ... troubles ... troubles ...
> Primitive ... grave ... evils ... curses ...
> (*A middle-aged, somewhat robot-like* WORKING MAN *comes on followed by his* WIFE. *They approach the* MAD KING.)

WORKING MAN (*sings*).

> May we fall into conversation, Your Majesty?
> I'm a middle-aged working man, quite ordinary.
> Employed in a nationalized industry.
> (MAD KING *nods his gracious assent.*)
> Rainfall is quite as likely as snow,
> Were not the weather so sultry –

WORKING MAN AND WIFE (*sing angrily*).

> If we had the money to go
> We wouldn't stay in this country.

MAD KING (*sings*).

> Come, come, there's always a change in the weather
> And even this government can't last for ever.

WORKING MAN (*sings*).

> I have two point four children, grammar school children,
> Two of them married now, with families.
> But I won't be happy till all my children
> Live with their offspring overseas.
> For in fifteen or twenty years' time,
> Fifteen or twenty years' time,
> The Blakes will have the whip-hand
> Over the non-Blake man.
>
> (WORKING MAN *and* WIFE *wave as their* CHILDREN *depart on an ocean liner, waving little Union Jacks.* MAD KING *wipes away a tear.*)

MAD KING (*sings*).

> Here is a decent ordinary Englishman
> Talking to his King in broad daylight.
> His children have fled from their own native country.
> I cannot shrug my shoulders
> I do not have the right.
> For what he is saying
> Thousands and hundreds of thousands are saying.
>
> (*Enter* CHORUS OF THE PEOPLE OF BRITAIN.)

CHORUS (*sing indignantly*).

> In fifteen or twenty years there will be in Britain
> Millions of William Blakes and their children.
> In the year two thousand there'll be seven million,
> About one-tenth of the total population ...
>
> (*Enter* SCOFIELD, *with* Jerusalem *under his arm, followed by* SOLDIERS *in dark red uniforms and modern riot equipment.*)

MAD KING (*sings*).

> Evils ... aliens ...

SCOFIELD (*sings*).

> Those whom the gods wish to destroy
> They first make mad.
> We must be mad, literally mad –

MAD KING (*sings*).

>We must be mad, literally mad –

CHORUS (*sing*).

>We must be mad, literally mad –
>Strangers in our own land.
>Our wives giving birth with no hospital bed.
>Our plans and our prospects defeated.
>Our homes and our neighbourhoods changed out of all
>recognition.

MAD KING. My loyally cringing subjects and objects. I would like you all to open your hearts tonight. For we have among us one who has suffered atrociously at the barbaric hands of the Blake people. And here she is – to tell her tragedy in her own unrehearsed words – The Widow of Wolverhampton!

>(*Enter* SIR JOSHUA *dressed as the Widow.*)

SIR JOSHUA (*sings*).

>My husband and my two sons were lost in the war.
>My only asset was a house with a mortgage.
>I used it as a boarding house and worked very hard
>To put something by for my old age.

CHORUS (*sing*).

>A respectable house
>In a respectable street
>In Wolverhampton, Wolverhampton.

SIR JOSHUA. Then the Blake people moved in.

>(*Sings.*)
>I saw the other houses taken over,
>Fear growing every day.
>Regretfully, regretfully,
>My non-Blake tenants moved away.
>
>I was woken at seven as I lay in my house alone
>By two William Blakes who wanted to use my phone.

I refused
I was abused
And I feared I would have been struck to the floor
Were it not for the chain on my front door.

Now, afraid to go out,
Windows broken by rocks,
I find William Blake excreta
Pushed through my letter-box ...
(SIR JOSHUA, *as Widow, breaks into sobs.*)

MAD KING (*sings with mighty menace*).
A cloud no bigger than the hand of a man
Can overcast the sky.
I saw that cloud over Wolverhampton
Spreading rapidly.

SCOFIELD (*sings*).
Filled with foreboding by this great betrayal
I pledge myself to battle with this tragic flood.
For, like the Roman, I seem to see
The River Tiber flowing with blood,
The River Tiber flowing with blood.

CHORUS, MAD KING AND SIR JOSHUA (*sing mightily*).
We pledge ourselves to belabour and batter
The head of William Blake,
And the blood of Blake shall flow until
It forms a scarlet lake.
And then we'll get in our yachts and hold a regatta
On the blood of William Blake.

MAD KING. We've rejected him, neglected him, investigated him and threatened him. And yet he continues to breathe and paint and poem and reproduce himself after his own kind of kind kind.

(SCOFIELD, *now a Captain, enters, kneels and presents* MAD KING *with the large volume which he stole from* BLAKE.)

78

MAD KING. Yes?

SCOFIELD. Captain Scofield, sire.

MAD KING. What's this?

SCOFIELD. A book, your majesty.

MAD KING. Yes, yes, a book, thank you, Captain. (*Holding book distastefully.*) Look, Josh, a book. What book is this?

SCOFIELD (*sardonically*). A veritable mountain of a book, sir – called *Jerusalem*. It appears, Your Majesty, that Oxford Street is in Jerusalem.

SIR JOSHUA. You might as soon find Jesus Christ in Mark's and Spencer. Ha ha ha.

MAD KING. Yes. Ha ha ha. But Josh, Josh, what shall I do with this book thing?

SIR JOSHUA. Why, open it, Your Majesty. Like this. (*Opens the book. Golden smoke pours out.*)

CHORUS (*sing*).

> For everything that lives is holy.
>
> For everything that lives is holy.
>
> (SOLDIERS *appear in deep-red riot uniforms and batter the book to death. Singing stops, then resumes from the auditorium.*)

CHORUS (*sing*).

> For everything that lives is holy.
>
> For everything that lives is holy.
>
> (SOLDIERS *lie down and open fire on the audience.*)

MAD KING. That's the style, my bloody-coated men. Shoot 'em down, gas 'em, then shoot 'em down again.

> (MAD KING *pulls cross from orb with his teeth and throws orb like a grenade.*)

FIRST SOLDIER (*to* SECOND SOLDIER). What sort of fire-power have those monkeys got, Jim?

CHORUS (*sing*).

> For everything that lives is holy.

79

SECOND SOLDIER. Can't tell. Looks like they're just sitting down behind the barricades.

CHORUS (*sing*).

For everything that lives is holy.

SCOFIELD. I want you chaps to remember that we're here to maintain –

SOLDIERS. Law and order.

SCOFIELD. So you'll bear in mind that there's one priority, and one priority only –

CHORUS (*sing*).

For everything that lives is holy.

SOLDIERS. Kill the buggers.

(*A big burst of firing.* KATE, *wounded, staggers onto the stage. She falls in a heap and lies there, ignored.*)

MAD KING. All right, that'll do. Cease fire and back to your kennels.

(SOLDIERS *disperse.*)

Captain!

(SCOFIELD *goes to* MAD KING.)

SCOFIELD. Your Mad Majesty?

MAD KING. How many buggers dead?

SCOFIELD. Three buggers dead and fifteen wounded, sir.

MAD KING (*tapping* SCOFIELD *on the shoulder with his sceptre*).

Arise, Sir Captain Scofield. Didn't we meet somewhere before? In some devastated place?

SCOFIELD. Correct, your Majesty. You were kind enough to award me the Massacre Medal after the recent subjugation.

MAD KING. Now, who wrote that alleged book? Riot fodder.

SCOFIELD. That book was made by William Blake.

MAD KING. The screwy scribbler strikes again! Right, Scofield, enough is too much! Bring Blake to me dead or alive or half way in between.

(*Exit* SCOFIELD.)

B-L-A-K-E spells trouble.

SIR JOSHUA.   They seek him here, they seek him there,
The scholars seek him everywhere.
Is he a mystic or a mistake
This damned ubiquitous William Blake?

MAD KING. Oh, who will rid me of this tumescent beast?

SIR JOSHUA. He's a moon-maniac, that's what he is.

MAD KING. Josh, that's it. Josh, you've done it. For the first time in your grovelling life, you've done it. What a schemer you are? And what a plan!

SIR JOSHUA. But what's this plan of mine?

MAD KING. We'll send Blake to the moon.

SIR JOSHUA. In a British rocket.

MAD KING. Aha. Ha. Ha. Then he'll never come back. I like it. I like it. Yes, and I'll be fair. People do still have friends, don't they? Right. He can pick some friends to help him.

SIR JOSHUA. A team.

MAD KING. Yes, a bit of teamwork. That's what made Britain, er, Britain.

(SCOFIELD *enters. Two* SOLDIERS *bring on* BLAKE, *who has been beaten up, and fling him down beside* KATE. BLAKE *sits her up, ties a handkerchief round her wound, and helps her to stand during the next few speeches.*)

MAD KING. Mr Blake – they tell me that you are mad, bad and dangerous to quote. Mr Blake, you are causing disturbances to my loyal. Mr Blake, you know damn well I could throw the Domesday Book at you, let alone the Doomsday Machine –

BLAKE (*savagely*).

Cruelty has a Human Heart,
And Jealousy a Human Face;
Terror the Human Form Divine,
And Secrecy the Human Dress.

The Human Dress is forged Iron,

81

> The Human Form a fiery Forge,
> The Human Face a Furnace seal'd,
> The Human Heart its hungry Gorge.

MAD KING. But I'm a *merciful* King –

SIR JOSHUA. Ain't that the truth –

MAD KING. I'm a just King –

SIR JOSHUA. Tell it like it was –

MAD KING. And I'm a mad King, shut up, Josh, and I've decided that you shall be privileged to go on a royally-sponsored jaunt to the moon.

(*A huge rocket is lowered on to the stage.*)

BLAKE. We'll take off in your Satanic contraption. But once we're out of your atmosphere, we'll jettison every last rivet. And we'll touch down on the moon in a craft of my own design.

MAD KING. Right Blake, choose your Mission Controllers.

BLAKE. I'll take Henry Fuseli and Sam Palmer.

(*Enter* FUSELI *and* PALMER. *While they confer with* BLAKE, SIR JOSHUA, *with microphone, beckons to* KATE *and interviews her.*)

SIR JOSHUA. Mrs Blake, as your husband prepares to enter the royal rocket, what thoughts do you suppose are struggling and scintillating in the amazing if obtuse mind of William Blake?

KATE. I expect he's wondering how to survive.

SIR JOSHUA. How to survive? Yes. How to *survive*.

KATE. At least I hope he is.

SIR JOSHUA. And I'm sure that billions of viewers tonight are sharing that hope – that faith, that *prayer*, because it is a prayer, Mrs Blake, isn't it?

KATE. He'll be singing to himself. And getting ready to look at the universe. His eyes are very big, you know. Abnormally big eyes. And when he sees something that pleases his eyes, well, they open very large and round.

82

SIR JOSHUA. Perhaps you could give me an example –

KATE. Well, when we moved down into the country, by the seaside, you know, out of London, so Mr Blake could do his true work, which is creating, there was a moment like that. The first morning down there in the country, Mr Blake went for a walk. And there was a ploughman and a plough-boy. And the ploughboy said to the ploughman: 'Father, the gate is open.' And when Mr Blake told me about that I looked at his eyes. And they were very big.

SIR JOSHUA. That's very moving, Mrs Blake, if entirely meaningless to me. But what do you suppose are the reactions of your husband as he prepares to confront the naked universe?

KATE. I expect he's crying.

SIR JOSHUA. And what do you feel at this moment, Mrs Blake?

KATE. Fear and trembling. How about you? Excuse me, I've got to go now.

> (BLAKE and KATE enter the rocket. FUSELI and PALMER establish themselves with microphones at either side of the stage.)

MAD KING. Ten – nine – eight – seven – six – five – four – three – two – one – zero – inspiration – blast off!

> (SIR JOSHUA and MAD KING exit. The rocket blasts off, out of sight. It reveals a golden circular carpet on the stage. On the carpet is a Moon-Ark based on the design in Blake's Jerusalem – a small ark with golden feathered wings. There is a ladder at one end of the Moon-Ark. BLAKE appears on the deck.)

FUSELI. Is the pressure about right? (Pause) Hello, this is Fuseli at Lambeth Ground Control calling Albion One. Do you read me? Is there too much pressure?

BLAKE. This is the hatching. Hatching from the wooden egg. My flesh and blood and bone are all like egg-yolk. How's an embryo supposed to know the right moment to be born?

PALMER. Don't get born until you have to.

FUSELI. We're getting an impossible reading on your heart. Is there some kind of moonquake up on that artichoke? How are you going? Over.

BLAKE. Fear and trembling. Fear and trembling.

PALMER. Then you'll do.

FUSELI. Ground Control to Bright Red Son of the New Dawn. Getting a good picture. Over.

BLAKE. This is the lamb with teeth speaking. It's easier than it seems. I repeat, it's harder than it looks.

PALMER. This is the Ground speaking. The Fourfold Vision Camera is A.O.K.

BLAKE. I think we might be able to make it here. I think we might –

FUSELI. The reading on your portable life supply consumables says you've got just about enough to get by on.

BLAKE. Never asked any more than that. I'm standing on the bottom rung now. Just trying the surface with the tip of my boot. Sort of fine, golden ... Here goes the first foot. Sinks in a little way ... Dusty carpet ... Here's the other foot. I'm letting go now. Yes, it's possible to stand up.

> My mother groan'd, my father wept,
> Into the dangerous world I leapt,
> Helpless, naked, piping loud,
> Like a fiend hid in a cloud.

FUSELI. What are the instruments saying? Sad or happy? Happy or sad?

KATE (*appearing on the deck of the Moon-Ark*). Both.

BLAKE (*sings to himself*).

> He who binds to himself a joy
> Does the winged life destroy;
> But he who kisses the joy as it flies
> Lives in eternity's sun rise.

FUSELI. Listen, Tyger, this is Operation Jerusalem.

PALMER. The schedule's tight.

84

FUSELI. Keep the data flowing.

PALMER. We need pictures. We need words.

FUSELI. We need everything you have.

BLAKE. I'm a builder. I want to start building.

PALMER. Hey, I thought the happy pills were only for emergencies.

KATE. This man's whole life is an emergency.

(BLAKE *looks around him, then stops.*)

BLAKE. I can see them. I can see them. Get down here, Kate.

KATE (*as* CHILD *appears from inside Moon-Ark*). Come on, Bill (*or Joy, depending on the child's sex*). The moon's a good place.

(KATE *brings the* CHILD *to* BLAKE.)

BLAKE. We can see them now.

PALMER. Who are they?

BLAKE. The Children of Albion. The people. The ordinary people, who are all extraordinary. My brothers and sisters. And the Wretched of the Earth. Revolutionaries, all with their own visions of the Revolution. These are the children of the New Age, which begins today. These are the Builders of Jerusalem.

(CHORUS, *men and woman, emerge from the sides of the stage and from the orchestra. They carry dark wooden shapes, mostly objects used as furniture earlier in the play. During the two songs which follow,* BLAKE *and* KATE, FUSELI *and* PALMER *join the* CHORUS *in piling up these objects until gradually they form a dark city, somewhat in the shape of a hill town.* CHORUS *should concentrate on building the city rather than moving in time to the music. Their work sets the pace and rhythm of their movements. This is* not *a ritual, but a job of work, so if necessary builders can consult quietly with each other about which bit to put on next.*

During this work, enormous slides of pages from the illuminated books of BLAKE, *especially* Jerusalem, *are projected. It won't be possible to read the words, but that's not the idea.*)

85

As work begins, ISABELLE *comes forward.*)
ISABELLE (*sings*).

The fields from Islington to Marybone,
To Primrose Hill and Saint John's Wood,
Were builded over with pillars of gold,
And there Jerusalem's pillars stood.

Her Little-ones ran on the fields,
The Lamb of God among them seen,
And fair Jerusalem his Bride,
Among the little meadows green.

Pancras & Kentish-town repose
Among her golden pillars high,
Among her golden arches which
Shine upon the starry sky.

The Jew's-harp-house & the Green Man,
The Ponds where Boys to bathe delight,
The fields of Cows by Willan's farm,
Shine in Jerusalem's pleasant sight ...

In my Exchanges every Land
Shall walk, & mine in every Land,
Mutual shall build Jerusalem,
Both heart & hand in hand.

I see thy Form, O lovely mild Jerusalem, Wing'd with Six
    Wings
In the opacous Bosom of the Sleeper, lovely Three-fold,
In Head & Heart & Reins, three Universes of love &
    beauty.
Thy forehead bright, Holiness to the Lord, with Gates of
    pearl
Reflects Eternity; beneath, thy azure wings of feathery
    down

Ribb'd delicate & cloth'd with feather'd gold & azure &
    purple,
From thy white shoulders shadowing purity in holiness!
Thence, feather'd with soft crimson of the ruby, bright as
    fire,
Spreading into the azure, Wings which like a canopy
Bends over thy immortal Head in which Eternity dwells.
(*The* CHORUS, *the* BLAKES, PALMER *and* FUSELI *paint
the city gold, but continue to build. When the song is over, the
projections from the illuminated books cease.*)
BLAKE. England! awake! awake! awake!
    (*The Builders of Jerusalem continue their work. The band
    plays.*)

CURTAIN